Information Literacy Toolkit

GRADES KINDERGARTEN–6

JENNY RYAN

STEPH CAPRA

AMERICAN LIBRARY ASSOCIATION
Chicago and London   2001

Consulting editor, Donald A. Adcock

Cover design by Megan Hibberd, Kean Design, Eight Mile Plains, Q. Australia

The paper used in this publication meets the minimum requirements of American National Standard for Information Sciences—Permanence of Paper for Printed Library Materials, ANSI Z39.48-1992. ∞

Library of Congress Cataloging-in-Publication Data
Ryan, Jenny, 1955-
  Information literacy toolkit. Grades kindergarten-6 / Jenny Ryan and Steph Capra.
    p.   cm.
  Includes bibliographical references and index.
  ISBN 0-8389-3507-9 (alk. paper)
  1. Information literacy—Study and teaching (Elementary)—United States. 2. Information resources—Evaluation—Study and teaching (Elementary)—United States. I. Capra, Steph. II. Title

  ZA3075.R93 2001
  372.6–dc21   00-052166

Printed in the United States of America

05   04   5   4   3

To our ever-supportive families:
the two Petes, Carlie, Dave,
Michelle, Kris, John,
and Leon

Contents

Acknowledgments

Our special thanks to the following for their continuing support, encouragement, and valued professional contribution:

Michelle Young,
St. Rita's Primary School,
Victoria Point

Raylee Elliott-Burns,
Brisbane Catholic Education

Karen Bonanno,
Karen Bonanno & Associates

Robyn Hindmarsh,
Mary MacKillop Catholic
Primary School

Brian Armour,
Redlands College

Jan Barnett,
St. Lawrence's College

Clare Burford,
St. Joseph's, Nudgee

Kerryl Fleming,
John Paul College

Anne Green,
Redeemer Lutheran College

Joan Jenkins,
St. Aidan's School

Maryanne Salisbury,
Runcorn State High School

Fraser-Cooloola District
Technology Group

And to Jamie McKenzie,
whose words of wisdom
and encouragement were
inspirational.

We thank you.

Introduction

Educators of the twenty-first century now face the challenge of preparing learners and workers for the information age. With the societal shift from an industrial model to an information model comes the emphasis on information literacy skills. People must be able to think critically, use learning technologies, and access and use information to participate effectively in society. It is necessary to learn the skills of "learning how to learn" to become lifelong learners.

For many years, academics and researchers have struggled to find a definition for the term "information literacy." While the definitions themselves may vary somewhat, a consistent common thread is the notion that information literacy encompasses critical thinking and problem solving as well as the ethical use of information. We have adopted the definition of information literacy from the "Final Report" of the American Library Association Presidential Committee on Information Literacy:

> To be information literate, a person must be able to recognize when information is needed and have the ability to locate, evaluate, and use effectively the needed information.[1]

In 1998, the American Association of School Libraries (AASL) and the Association for Educational Communications and Technology (AECT) published *Information Power: Building Partnerships for Learning,* which identified the stages of information problem solving as being the key elements of an information literacy curriculum.[2] It also identified the benefits of the library media specialist working collaboratively with teachers to integrate information literacy into the curriculum. This partnership helps facilitate the change from textbook-based learning to resource-based learning—an approach that uses a variety of resources. Resource-based learning is an essential component of an information literacy program that supports the acquisition of lifelong learning skills.

Another book by AASL and AECT, *Information Literacy Standards for Student Learning,* groups the information literacy standards in three broad categories: information literacy, independent learning, and social responsibility.[3] The book provides three levels of proficiency—basic, proficient, and exemplary—to gauge the mastery of each information literacy standard.

It is this holistic approach to information literacy that is crucial to the development of individuals who will contribute positively to society and contribute to the economic development of this country. The emphasis on independent learning culminating in social responsibility may be achieved through a structured-process approach to the teaching of information literacy.

Information Power also acknowledged and supported the integral role of the library media specialist in the development of information literacy in students. As a collaborative partner providing sustained professional input, the library media specialist helps create a rich learning environment.

Integrating information technology skills into the curriculum using the information literacy process outlined in this *Information Literacy Toolkit* is an educationally sound means for students to acquire computer skills. In fact, the International Society for Technology in Education's publication *National Educational Technology: Standards for Students* clearly links the skills of computer literacy to those found in the process overviews in part 1 of the *Toolkit.*[4] Teaching these literacy skills in a cohesive manner is a critical factor in achieving information literacy behaviors in students. Developing these skills to create lifelong learners and socially responsible members of society is the ultimate goal of educators across all curriculum areas. The *Information Literacy Toolkit: Grades Kindergarten–6* was developed to address the issue of supporting educators in teaching lifelong-learning skills. A process approach to teaching these skills forms the basis for the information literacy program.

The Vision

The use of the *Information Literacy Toolkit* provides a powerful model to integrate national and state standards into curriculum planning. It is a focal planning tool for teachers and library media specialists.

Linking information literacy with unit or subject areas, these planning tools integrate information literacy into the curriculum across all subject areas. By using the forms provided when planning curricula, skills can be taught that may have previously been thought difficult to integrate. The structure of the *Toolkit* provides a base on which to build knowledge of information literacy. It is crucial to include the entire six-stage process rather than individual skills because each skill forms part of the total process. Students need to achieve a high degree of understanding that it is this process approach to learning that provides them with behaviors for lifelong learning.

The *Information Literacy Toolkit* facilitates curriculum planning. With the accompanying CD-ROM, the *Toolkit* forms the basis on which to create a comprehensive, cohesive, and sequentially developed school-based information literacy program.

The *Toolkit* has three major components:

1. process overviews with a scope and sequence listing of the progressive skills for each of the six stages of the process
2. planning organizers for use when determining the year's curriculum units
3. teaching tools to draw from for information literacy process activities applicable to the units of study

Information literacy is a six-stage process. The flexible structure of the process makes it applicable as a planning tool for any process approach to teaching information literacy, e.g., Big6, etc.

Links from *Information Literacy Standards for Student Learning* to the *Toolkit*

As stated previously, AASL's *Information Literacy Standards for Student Learning* provides national guidelines for information literacy and identifies three categories of learning—information literacy, independent learning, and social responsibility. The *Toolkit* skills found in part 1, "Process Overviews," articulate a sequential and developmental program that encompasses AASL's standards in a flexible teacher-planning format. The nine standards follow.

Information Literacy

Standard 1: The student who is information literate accesses information efficiently and effectively.

Standard 2: The student who is information literate evaluates information critically and competently.

Standard 3: The student who is information literate uses information accurately and creatively.

Independent Learning

Standard 4: The student who is an independent learner is information literate and pursues information related to personal interests.

Standard 5: The student who is an independent learner is information literate and appreciates literature and other creative expressions of information.

Standard 6: The student who is an independent learner is information literate and strives for excellence in information seeking and knowledge generation.

Social Responsibility

Standard 7: The student who contributes positively to the learning community and to society is information literate and recognizes the importance of information to a democratic society.

Standard 8: The student who contributes positively to the learning community and to society is information literate and practices ethical behavior in regard to information and information technology.

Standard 9: The student who contributes positively to the learning community and to society is information literate and participates effectively in groups to pursue and generate information.[5]

The skills identified in the *Toolkit* will assist in the development of students as socially responsible members of society. By using a process approach, students have the opportunity to practice the skills of

- critical thinking and problem solving
- being socially responsible participants within society

The ability to solve problems will prepare students for an information-based society and a workplace centered on technology. To develop skills in problem solving and to overcome the problem of plagiarism, students must be given the opportunity to offer original solutions to a problem. By framing a unit of work as a problem or task, rather than a topic, students have the opportunity to create and present original ideas as opposed to simply reading and regurgitating the knowledge of others.

Sequentially developed skills provide opportunities for students to acquire attitudes and behaviors relating to the ethical use of information. The information literacy program provides sustained opportunities for students to become socially responsible, active participants in society.

The School-Wide Initiative

A whole-school approach to integrating information literacy across grades K–12 will result in students' exposure to a comprehensive development of skills and competency in the use of a process approach to problem solving. The CD-ROM that accompanies the *Toolkit* can be used to create a whole-school document.

You can achieve maximum staff ownership if staff cooperatively complete and modify their own planning documents. Subsequent whole-staff discussion and modification of the resulting planners, commencing with the lowest level and progressing to the highest, enable teachers to understand the sequential and developmental nature of the information literacy program.

The process of adapting the program will be ongoing to meet changing curriculum needs. It may take schools up to twelve months using and modifying the initial planning organizers to reflect the elements of the school's requirements. All skills, particularly those of computer literacy, will require adaptation to school circumstances.

How to Use the *Toolkit*

Part 1 of the *Toolkit* defines the six stages of the information literacy process and shows the progression of skills for each stage across grade levels. It is recommended that all teachers and library media specialists be given a copy of this part and read through it to develop an awareness of the scope and progression of the information literacy skills. If necessary, adjustments can be made to the level of difficulty of skills for a grade level; however, make sure that the integrity of the sequential and developmental nature of the skills is retained. Through this effort it is possible to see what has come before and what the present skills lead to at the next level, giving an overview of the entire process.

Part 2 pulls the skills together for individual grades. Use the planning organizers at the beginning of the school year to map out the units of the curriculum for the year and to connect the information literacy skills to that curriculum. If at all possible, this should be a collaborative effort by teachers and library media specialists so that information literacy can be sequentially integrated into learning activities and assessment tasks. With systematic planning, all skills are covered for each grade level.

Part 3 includes a variety of teaching tools that are applicable across grades and curriculum units. The unit planner found in this part helps you organize the skills, activities, assessment measures, and resources wanted for use with a unit. The introduction provides guidance for framing units as problems to be solved or tasks to be accomplished. It also offers examples of ways to embed technology into the information literacy process.

The planning organizers in part 2 and teaching tools in part 3 of the *Information Literacy Toolkit* may be photocopied for use within a school. These forms are protected by copyright. The publisher and author grant *Information Literacy Toolkit* users the right to reproduce the forms, whether copied as-is or adapted for nonprofit purposes within a single school setting on the condition that the publisher's source line appears on each page. The standard source line included on the documents provided in the book is

The documents in parts 1 and 2 were prepared in Microsoft Excel 97. For convenience in customizing the files to individual school settings, those files are provided on the CD-ROM at the back of the book. Users who are supplementing these documents with their own material may use the source line:

NOTES

1. American Library Assn. Presidential Committee on Information Literacy, "Final Report" (Chicago: American Library Assn., 1989), 1. Available: http://www.ala.org/acrl/nili/ilit1st.html

2. American Assn. of School Librarians and Assn. for Educational Communications and Technology, *Information Power: Building Partnerships for Learning* (Chicago: American Library Assn., 1998).

3. American Assn. of School Librarians and Assn. for Educational Communications and Technology, *Information Literacy Standards for Student Learning* (Chicago: American Library Assn., 1998), 8–9.

4. International Society for Technology in Education, *National Educational Technology Standards for Students* (Eugene, Ore.: The Society, 1998).

5. American Assn. of School Librarians and Assn. for Educational Communications and Technology, *Information Literacy Standards*, 8–9.

1

Process Overviews

The overviews for each stage of the information literacy process give a broad view of the progression of skills from the lowest to highest degree of competency. The six stages of the process are defined in the following statements to ensure a common understanding. Other terms can be substituted if you are using another process model, while keeping the integrity of the actual process.

1. *Defining* The student formulates questions and analyzes and clarifies the requirements of the problem or task. This is the first stage in the information literacy cycle. As a result of new learnings and understandings, this stage is constantly revisited during the entire process to refine and redefine the problem or task for further clarification.

2. *Locating* The student identifies potential sources of information and locates and accesses a variety of resources using multiple formats.

3. *Selecting/analyzing* The student analyzes, selects, and rejects information from the located resources appropriate to the problem or task.

4. *Organizing/synthesizing* The student critically analyzes and organizes the gathered information, synthesizes new learnings incorporating prior knowledge, and develops original solutions to a problem or task.

5. *Creating/presenting* The student creates an original response to the problem or task and presents the solution to an appropriate audience.

6. *Evaluating* The student critically evaluates the effectiveness of his or her ability to complete the requirements of the task and identifies future learning needs.

The skills contained in each stage of the overview have been extensively benchmarked and validated against national and international standards. Attainment levels for each student continue at an individual rate within a range but generally approximate the relevant year level.

Each new skill, whether a first introduction or an incrementally harder skill, is shown in bold in the overviews. Skills already experienced at the same level of complexity as the previous level are shown in regular type.

Within the stages, each skill progresses with decreasing levels of teaching support. The terminology reflects the level of teaching support required:

- "Modeled examples/techniques" is used when a skill is first introduced and has a high level of teacher input and support and the skill is specifically taught.
- "With guidance" reflects the second level of support in which the teacher maintains accessible support for the student—the teacher is the "guide on the side."
- Skills without qualifiers indicate that students are assumed to have competency in this skill, so there is little or no need for direct teacher support.

Give a full set of the process overviews along with the planning organizers to each teacher at the beginning of the academic year. This facilitates the teacher's understanding of the sequential and developmental nature of the skills and this is especially important in ensuring the continuity of the teaching of information literacy in the school.

Information Literacy Planning Organizer K–6
Overview of Defining Stage

Kindergarten. Through planned learning activities the student:
discusses a given topic in response to an audio and/or visual stimulus
draws on prior knowledge to brainstorm ideas and vocabulary for a given question
understands and uses terminology: title, author, illustrator, spine, spine label

Grade 1. Through planned learning activities the student:
discusses a given topic in response to an audio and/or visual stimulus
draws on prior knowledge to brainstorm ideas and vocabulary for a given question
categorizes information into lists (written or graphic)
brainstorms possible sources of new information
understands and uses terminology: title, author, illustrator, spine, spine label

Grade 2. Through planned learning activities the student:
discusses a given topic in response to an audio and/or visual stimulus
draws on prior knowledge to brainstorm key ideas and vocabulary for a given question
uses key ideas to formulate focus questions using teacher-modeled examples
categorizes information into lists (written or graphic)
brainstorms possible sources of new information
understands and uses terminology: title, author, illustrator, spine, spine label

Grade 3. Through planned learning activities the student:
discusses a given topic in response to an audio and/or visual stimulus
draws on prior knowledge to brainstorm key ideas and vocabulary for a topic
understands the organizing principle of main heading
devises focus questions in groups using modeled examples
organizes focus questions into headings from clustered ideas using modeled examples
contributes to a teacher-devised search plan which lists:
  headings
  key words and possible search terms
  focus questions
  likely sources of information
understands and uses terminology: publisher, series, contents, index

Grade 4. Through planned learning activities the student:
draws on prior knowledge to brainstorm key ideas and vocabulary for a topic
devises focus questions in groups and individually using modeled examples
organizes focus questions into headings from clustered ideas with guidance
contributes to a teacher-devised search plan which lists:
  headings
  key words and possible search terms
  focus questions
  likely sources of information

Information Literacy Planning Organizer K–6
Overview of Defining Stage

Grade 5. Through planned learning activities the student:

draws on prior knowledge to brainstorm and cluster ideas with teachers and peers

analyzes and clarifies a given task using modeled techniques

devises focus questions in groups and individually using modeled examples

organizes focus questions into headings from clustered ideas with guidance

prepares a group search plan which lists:

   headings

   key words and possible search terms

   focus questions

   likely sources of information

Grade 6. Through planned learning activities the student:

develops appropriate questioning techniques through extensive modeling to clarify requirements of task

analyzes and clarifies a given task with guidance

selects from a range of topics using modeled techniques

draws on prior knowledge to brainstorm and cluster ideas with guidance

identifies and interprets key words in task using modeled techniques

develops focus questions using modeled techniques

prepares a simple search plan which lists:

   headings and subheadings

   key words and possible search terms

   focus questions

   likely sources of information

Information Literacy Planning Organizer K–6
Overview of Locating Stage

Kindergarten. Through planned learning activities the student:

is aware of layout of kindergarten and library

knows location of easy fiction and type of books housed there

understands easy fiction resources are housed in a particular order

learns borrowing procedures of school resources

uses software icon menu on desktop

uses keyboard—use of mouse and cursor (point and double clicking)
   Enter/Return key, locate and click, mouse pad, monitor

interacts with story using mouse

is aware of the Internet as a resource, especially e-mail

Grade 1. Through planned learning activities the student:

is aware of layout of classroom, library and school

knows location of easy fiction and type of books found there

is aware that easy fiction is shelved in alphabetical order according to last name of author

learns borrowing procedures for school resources

differentiates between fiction and nonfiction resources and their location

is aware of primary resources as a source of information, e.g., first-hand experience, people, concrete objects

is aware of secondary resources as a source of information, e.g., book, pictures, AV materials

is aware of computer system skills using modeled examples:
   can turn computer on
   uses terminology—monitor, keyboard, mouse, disk drive, printer, disk, CD-ROM
   understands and uses keyboard—space bar, Enter/Return, caps lock
   interacts with story using mouse
   practices hand and finger placement on keyboard
   uses file menu to exit program

is aware of the Internet and e-mail as a communication tool and information source

Grade 2. Through planned learning activities the student:

is aware of layout of library and school

differentiates between fiction and nonfiction sections of the library and uses the spine label to identify resources

is aware that nonfiction resources are shelved according to classification order

finds resources in both school library and public libraries with assistance

is aware of primary resources as a source of information, e.g., first-hand experience, people, concrete objects

is aware of secondary resources as a source of information, e.g., book, pictures, AV materials, magazines

begins to use contents and index pages of nonfiction books using key words

is aware of computer system skills through modeled examples by:
   saving into appropriate folders/directories
   retrieving saved document
   being able to turn computer on/off correctly
   using file menu to exit program
   understands and uses keyboard—space bar, Enter/Return, mouse, cursor, locate and click, caps lock
   is aware of finger placement on keyboard home keys

acquires information from different instructional displays

is aware of search strategies to help select and locate resources

is aware of the Internet (e-mail) as a communication tool and information source

Grade 3. Through planned learning activities the student:

follows a search plan with assistance

locates fiction using spine label

locates nonfiction using Dewey decimal classification system

locates appropriate resources in both school library and public libraries with assistance

begins to use contents and index pages of nonfiction books by using key words

Grade 3 [cont]. Through planned learning activities the student:

begins to identify primary and secondary sources of information

uses a range of resources as sources of information, e.g., encyclopedias, videos, CD-ROM

is aware of author, title or subject access to resources

is aware of key word searches using CD-ROM and online technology

using modeled examples, is aware of Internet/e-mail through:

    being aware of e-mail communication

    locating bookmarked Internet sites with assistance

    participating in online projects to locate, contribute and gather information

    starting browser software

    using back/forward navigation arrows in browser

    identifying and using links on a Web page

is aware of computer system skills using modeled examples by:

    saving into appropriate folders/directories

    retrieving saved document

    being able to turn computer on/off correctly

    reading and using software text and icon menu

    locating, reading and responding to software instructions

    interacting with story using mouse

understands the purpose of different displays and directional signage

locates and borrows magazines with assistance

Grade 4. Through planned learning activities the student:

follows a search plan with assistance

locates fiction using spine label

locates reference materials

uses reference tools—atlas, telephone book, encyclopedia, thesaurus, dictionary, reference CD-ROM

uses author, title, subject access in search strategies to identify the shelf label of a resource

using modeled examples, is aware of Internet/e-mail through:

    using e-mail as a form of communication and possible source of information

    locating bookmarked Internet sites with assistance

    participating in online projects to locate, contribute and gather information

    using back/forward navigation arrows in browser

is aware of computer system skills using modeled examples by:

    saving into appropriate folders/directories

    retrieving saved document

    using Save and Save as appropriately

    minimizing open documents/programs

identifies primary and secondary sources of information

locates appropriate resources using the Dewey decimal classification system

selects materials by scanning table of contents and assessing readability, presentation, and quality of illustrations

borrows magazines with assistance

is aware of key word searches using CD-ROM and online technology

locates reference materials, magazines, nonfiction, software, bookmarked Internet sites

uses reference books (encyclopedia, telephone directory) to locate information

uses author, title, subject, series to access resources through search strategies

identifies primary and secondary sources of information

gathers data from simple interviews, field trips, surveys, questionnaires

prejudges the relative worth of resources in terms of purpose

is aware of Internet search engines as a source of information

uses given Internet addresses with assistance

Information Literacy Planning Organizer K–6
Overview of Locating Stage

Grade 5. Through planned learning activities the student:

follows a search plan adding relevant information
locates reference materials, magazines, nonfiction, software, bookmarked Internet sites
uses reference books (encyclopedia, telephone directory) to locate information
uses author, title, subject, series to access resources
using modeled examples, extends use of Internet/e-mail by:
    using given Internet addresses with assistance
    bookmarking a location
    composing and sending e-mail
    accessing and reading e-mail
    replying to an e-mail message
    forwarding an e-mail message
    copying/pasting from Web page to document
    being aware of Internet search engines as a source of information
is aware of computer system skills using modeled examples by:
    saving into appropriate folders/directories
    retrieving saved document
    using Save and Save as appropriately
    minimizing open documents/programs
identifies primary and secondary sources of information
locates appropriate resources using the Dewey decimal classification system
gathers data from simple interviews, field trips, surveys, questionnaires
prejudges the relative worth of resources in terms of purpose
is aware of periodical indexes

Grade 6. Through planned learning activities the student:

follows a search plan using key words and related terms, modifying where necessary
determines the type of resource most appropriate for the topic
identifies and locates book and nonbook resources including:
    understanding organization of resources in school and local libraries
    recognizing the value of fiction for specific topics, e.g., historical fiction
    becoming familiar with limited number of appropriate search engines using modeled techniques
    using simple and combined terms to search catalog, Internet and CD-ROM sources
    choosing broader or narrower terms to refine search results
    using Help function to locate information and refine searches
    searching for information using given Internet addresses
    using information from the wider community
accesses periodical indexes using modeled techniques
identifies appropriate resources by
    using skimming and scanning techniques to survey readability in electronic and print resources
    using contents, index and text headings for all types of resources
with assistance, recognizes the differences in purpose and coverage of:
    magazines, newspaper, pamphlets, film, special reference materials, CD-ROM, Web searches, e-mail
recognizes where currency of information is necessary
recognizes the need to locate a variety of resources representing a range of views
with guidance, extends use of Internet/e-mail by:
    using given Internet addresses with assistance
    bookmarking a location
    composing and sending e-mail
    accessing and reading e-mail
    forwarding and replying to an e-mail message
    copying/pasting from Web page to document
    being aware of Internet search engines as a source of information
    being aware of Web page structure

Grade 6 [cont]. Through planned learning activities the student:

extends use of computer system skills using modeled examples by:
  deleting, copying, and moving files

identifies and locates information from both primary and secondary sources using modeled techniques

uses special print and non-print reference resources using modeled examples

uses index and knowledge of newspaper structure to select appropriate articles

uses key words, volume, index, and cross-references to find information in print and non-print encyclopedias

uses range of equipment to access information, e.g., telephone, fax, computer, scanner, digital camera using modeled techniques

uses e-mail to discuss topics and to facilitate cooperative activities using modeled examples

loads software for information retrieval

Information Literacy Planning Organizer K–6
Overview of Selecting/Analyzing Stage

Kindergarten.   Through planned learning activities the student:

uses pictures, objects, live specimens, etc., to extract information

selects books appropriate to interest using browsing techniques

responds to teacher-led discussion relating to pictures, objects, live specimens, etc.

interacts with resources through:

   following directions

   listening, observing and viewing

   identifying a sequence of ideas

   listening to and retelling stories in correct sequence

makes selections using simple scanning techniques involving cover and illustrations

makes simple decisions and justifies actions

Grade 1. Through planned learning activities the student:

selects books appropriate to interest and reading ability using browsing techniques

gains information through discussion using pictures, objects, live specimens, etc.

interacts with resources through:

   following directions

   listening, observing and viewing in response to focus questions

   identifying the main idea and key words

   identifying a sequence of ideas

   distinguishing between narrative and information texts

   listening to and retelling stories in correct sequence

makes selections using simple scanning techniques involving cover, title and illustrations

makes simple decisions and justifies actions

records relevant information using modeled examples by arranging ideas, events, and facts in sequence

   from oral, pictorial and written sources

constructs sentences orally using identified key words

is aware of people with special knowledge as a primary resource

Grade 2. Through planned learning activities the student

selects books appropriate to interest and reading ability using browsing techniques

gains information through discussion using pictures, objects, live specimens, etc.

compares different preselected resources on a topic deciding which is appropriate

makes selections using simple scanning techniques involving cover, title and illustrations

interacts with the resources through:

   following directions

   listening, observing and viewing in response to focus questions

   identifying the main idea and key words

   identifying a sequence of ideas

   distinguishing between narrative and information texts

   listening to and retelling stories in correct sequence

asks questions appropriately using modeled examples

records relevant information using modeled examples by:

   listing key words under main ideas

   arranging ideas, events and facts in sequence from oral, pictorial and written sources

constructs sentences orally using identified key words

is aware of people with special knowledge as a primary resource

Information Literacy Planning Organizer K–6
Overview of Selecting/Analyzing Stage

Grade 3. Through planned learning activities the student

selects books appropriate to interest and reading ability using browsing techniques

gains information through discussion using pictures, objects, live specimens, etc.

compares different preselected resources on a topic deciding which is appropriate

makes selections using simple scanning techniques involving cover, title and illustrations

interacts with the resources through:

    listening, observing and viewing in response to focus questions

    identifying the main idea and key words

    identifying a sequence of ideas

    distinguishing between narrative and information texts

    listening to and retelling stories in correct sequence

asks questions appropriately with guidance

records relevant information using modeled examples by:

    listing key words under main ideas

    arranging ideas, events and facts in sequence from oral, pictorial and written sources

    writing sentences using identified key words

is aware of people with special knowledge as a primary resource

Grade 4. Through planned learning activities the student

evaluates appropriateness of resources using modeled examples

uses appropriate note-taking templates using modeled examples

identifies and records relevant information from a resource by:

    using a note-taking strategy, e.g., listing

    clustering notes under subheadings

uses focus questions to identify key information and ideas from print and nonprint sources

compares information from different sources using modeled techniques

records bibliographic sources of information using author, title, publisher, date using modeled examples

is aware of a variety of primary and secondary sources using modeled examples

Grade 5. Through planned learning activities the student

selects resources using modeled techniques by:

    skimming and scanning

    using contents, index, and text headings

    using key words and key phrases

evaluates appropriateness of resources using modeled examples

modifies focus questions using modeled techniques

uses appropriate note-taking templates using modeled examples

identifies and records relevant information from a resource

records information using modeled examples by:

    using a note-taking strategy, e.g., concept mapping, outline, list making

    clustering notes under subheadings

makes simple comparisons between the purpose of different writing styles using modeled examples

analyzes consequences of group or community decision using modeled examples

compares information from different sources using modeled techniques

recognizes when a statement is a generalization

records bibliographic sources of information using author, title, publisher, date, http, date of download using modeled examples

uses a variety of primary and secondary sources using modeled examples

Information Literacy Planning Organizer K–6
Overview of Selecting/Analyzing Stage

Grade 6. Through planned learning activities the student

selects resources using modeled techniques by:

    skimming and scanning

    using contents, index, text headings, key words, and key phrases

evaluates appropriateness of resources using modeled examples

modifies focus questions using modeled techniques

devises appropriate note-taking templates using modeled examples

records information using modeled examples by:

    using a note-taking strategy, e.g., concept mapping, outline, list making

    clustering notes under subheadings

    selecting appropriate graphic organizer

understands that different accounts of the same event may vary

makes simple comparisons between the purpose of different writing styles using modeled examples

analyzes consequences of group or community decision

compares information from different sources using modeled techniques

is aware of the need for adequate data before drawing conclusions

records bibliographic sources of information using author, title, publisher, date, http, date of download using modeled examples

understands and complies with copyright requirements using modeled examples

observes netiquette conventions when communicating electronically using modeled techniques

understands there may be various interpretations of data

uses a variety of primary and secondary sources using modeled examples

Information Literacy Planning Organizer K–6
Overview of Organizing/Synthesizing Stage

Kindergarten. Through planned learning activities the student:
organizes oral/pictorial information in sequence
participates in teacher-led discussion
sorts objects according to different characteristics
begins to identify patterns and relationships using modeled examples
begins to think independently
begins to interact with peers in a fair manner
verifies results of experiments using modeled examples
practices hand and finger placement on keyboard
interacts with a variety of educational software
shares information with other children and adults

Grade 1. Through planned learning activities the student:
organizes oral/pictorial/written information in sequence
participates in teacher-led discussion to categorize information
sorts objects according to different characteristics
identifies patterns and relationships using modeled examples
begins to think independently
interacts with peers in a fair manner
participates in group discussion to propose a solution to a problem
verifies results of experiments using modeled examples
categorizes information into list format, both written and graphic
is introduced to the use of simple word processing through:
    an awareness of letters on keyboard, if interested and ready
    opening word processing application
    entering text, e.g., own name
    printing document
    an awareness of delete/backspace key
interacts with a variety of educational software
decides on an appropriate presentation format using modeled examples

Grade 2. Through planned learning activities the student:
participates in teacher-led discussion to categorize information
identifies patterns and relationships with guidance
recognizes the need for tolerance and respect for the opinions of peers
participates in group discussion to propose a solution to a problem
understands that ideas are more readily accepted if supported by sound reasoning
verifies results of experiments using modeled examples
categorizes information into list format, both written and graphic
using modeled examples, extends the use of word processing by:
    entering text—highlight, edit
    changing text—font/color, bold/italic/underline
    resizing text
    changing text alignment
has an awareness of letters on keyboard
decides on an appropriate presentation format using modeled examples

Information Literacy Planning Organizer K–6
Overview of Organizing/Synthesizing Stage

Grade 3. Through planned learning activities the student:
synthesizes selected information connecting similar ideas
recognizes the need for tolerance and respect for the opinions of peers
participates in group discussion to propose a solution to a problem
understands that ideas are more readily accepted if supported by sound reasoning
verifies results of experiments using modeled examples
categorizes information into list format
makes notes using modeled techniques, e.g., written bulleted points, note-taking template
using modeled examples, extends the use of word processing by:
   entering and editing text
   justifying text
   changing text—font/color, bold/italic/underline
   resizing text
   changing text alignment
   highlighting text
   saving
   printing
   using line spacing
   extends knowledge of finger placement on keyboard using both hands (left side, right side)
using modeled examples, is introduced to databases through:
   opening, browsing, and searching a commercial database, e.g., encyclopedia
decides on an appropriate presentation format using modeled examples

Grade 4. Through planned learning activities the student:
synthesizes selected information connecting similar ideas
participates in group discussion to propose a solution to a problem
verifies results of experiments using modeled examples
categorizes information according to a framework of headings using modeled examples
makes notes using modeled techniques, e.g., written bulleted points, note-taking template
using modeled examples, extends the use of word processing by:
   entering and editing text
   making notes using word processor or other software
   using Tab function
   understanding the difference between Cut and Copy
   copying selected text
   cutting and pasting text
   changes font size—before and after entering text
   practices posture and keyboard drills, e.g., hand and finger placement
using modeled examples, is introduced to databases through:
   opening, browsing, and searching a commercial database, e.g., encyclopedia
using modeled examples, is introduced to the use of spreadsheets by:
   opening a prepared spreadsheet
   entering data into specific cells
decides on an appropriate presentation format using modeled examples

Grade 5. Through planned learning activities the student:
synthesizes selected information connecting similar ideas and begins to predict possible outcomes
is aware there may be alternative solutions to a problem
uses information from various resources to support an argument
proposes a solution through group discussion to a set problem based on prior knowledge and new information that:
   organizes ideas and information logically
   makes simple generalizations and draws simple conclusions
verifies results of experiments using modeled examples

Information Literacy Planning Organizer K–6
Overview of Organizing/Synthesizing Stage

Grade 5 [cont]. Through planned learning activities the student:

categorizes information according to a framework of headings using modeled examples

makes notes using modeled techniques, e.g., written bulleted points, note-taking template, clipboards, etc.

using modeled examples, extends the use of word processing by:

  making notes using word processor or other software

  making notes directly from screen

  practicing keyboard drills, e.g., hand and finger placement

  using spell checker

  using columns

  changing page orientation (landscape/portrait)

  changing size of page, e.g., 75% view

  inserting graphics

  manipulating graphics, e.g., resizing

using modeled examples, is introduced to databases through:

  opening, browsing, and searching a commercial database, e.g., encyclopedia

using modeled examples, is introduced to the use of spreadsheets by:

  opening a prepared spreadsheet

  entering data into specific cells

recognizes information deficiencies

demonstrates sound reasoning when challenged

decides on an appropriate presentation format using modeled examples

Grade 6. Through planned learning activities the student:

using modeled examples, begins to discriminate between fact and opinion

synthesizes selected information connecting similar ideas and begins to predict possible outcomes

is aware there may be alternative solutions to a problem

uses information from various resources to support an argument

understands that comparisons must be based on similar characteristics

recognizes there may be various interpretations of data

engages in reflective thinking to analyze and clarify a problem

engages in group discussion to analyze and clarify a problem

proposes a solution to a set problem based on prior knowledge and new information which:

  organizes ideas and information logically

  makes simple generalizations and draws simple conclusions

verifies results of experiments using modeled examples

categorizes information according to a framework of headings and subheadings using modeled examples

selectively cuts and pastes information from an electronic source with guidance

  to quote a source

  to make notes

makes notes using modeled techniques, e.g., written bulleted points, note-taking template, clipboards, etc.

consolidates the use of word processing skills by:

  selectively cutting and pasting information from an electronic source with guidance

  making notes using word processor or other software

  making notes directly from screen

  using keyboard drills, Spelling, Grammar Check, Undo, Select all, Page Setup

  using lists/bullets

  creating and inserting simple tables

  wrapping text around graphics

  formatting text appropriate to text type

extends the use of databases using modeled examples through:

  browsing, editing, and adding records in a class-created database

  sorting and deleting records

  using Find function to search for specific criteria

Information Literacy Planning Organizer K–6
Overview of Organizing/Synthesizing Stage

Grade 6 [cont]. Through planned learning activities the student:

extends the use of spreadsheets by:
- **editing data in a prepared spreadsheet**
- **understanding the concept of a spreadsheet**
- **creating a new spreadsheet**
- **understanding the difference between columns and rows**
- **applying simple formulas—some digits (addition)**
- **formatting entries, e.g., bold**

recognizes information deficiencies and locates additional information using modeled examples

understands the need for sound reasoning when challenged

develops the ability to have faith in own judgment and point of view

decides on an appropriate presentation format using modeled examples

organizes ideas and information logically, e.g., time order, simple cause and effect

presents information using appropriate organizational frameworks with assistance, e.g.,
- **written and word-processed reports, recounts, procedures and lists**
- **using titles and subtitles appropriately**
- **oral reports, descriptions and comparisons supported by graphic and pictorial information**
- **construction such as models and displays, diagrams, and posters**
- **plays, role play**
- **desktop publishing (borders, WordArt, clip art)**
- **multimedia presentations using scanner, digital camera, video images and sound**

Information Literacy Planning Organizer K–6
Overview of Creating/Presenting Stage

Kindergarten. Through planned learning activities the student:

presents information in simple oral and visual sequence

presents a solution to a problem using a range of media, including:

   picture sequence, collage, mural, model and computer drawing

   dramatic presentations

enacts role play/puppet presentations

creates a response to a task/topic with assistance which uses information selected for the purpose

Grade 1. Through planned learning activities the student:

presents information in oral, written and visual sequence

presents a solution to a problem using a range of media, including:

   picture sequence, collage, mural, model and computer drawing

   dramatic presentations

begins to use Paint/Draw on computer with guidance:

   freehand drawing—pencil

   shape tools—box, circle

   selects objects with selection tool

   deletes selected objects

enacts role play/puppet presentations

creates a response to a task/topic which uses information selected for the purpose

presents word-processed document containing student's name and a sentence of text, printed with assistance

Grade 2. Through planned learning activities the student:

begins to understand the concept of "audience"

creates presentations exhibiting synthesis of information which:

   uses information appropriate to the task and the audience

   presents information in oral, written and visual sequence

presents a solution to a problem using a range of media, including:

   picture sequence, collage, mural, model and computer drawing

   dramatic presentations

uses Paint/Draw on computer with guidance including:

   drawing straight lines

   using eraser

   using shape tools

   using paintbrush/fill

presents word-processed document containing student's name and a paragraph of text, printed with assistance

Grade 3. Through planned learning activities the student:

begins to understand the concept of "audience"

creates presentations exhibiting synthesis of information that:

   uses information appropriate to the task and the audience

   organizes ideas and information logically, e.g., time sequence

presents a solution to a problem using:

   simple oral and written descriptions

   drawings

   constructions such as models or displays

   dramatic presentations

selectively prints presentations, e.g., word-processed paragraph

Information Literacy Planning Organizer K–6
Overview of Creating/Presenting Stage

Grade 3 [cont]. Through planned learning activities the student:

uses Paint/Draw with guidance including:
- drawing straight lines
- using eraser
- using shape tools
- using paintbrush/fill

Grade 4. Through planned learning activities the student:

understands the concept of "audience"

creates presentations exhibiting synthesis of information that:
- **uses logical structures such as time sequences, grids**
- uses information appropriate to the task and the audience

presents a solution to a problem using:
- simple oral and written reports
- **drawings, illustrations and simple bar graphs**
- **computer-generated drawings, illustrations and simple bar graphs which are labeled to summarize findings**
- constructions such as models or displays
- dramatic presentations
- **simple audio presentations**

using modeled examples, extends the use of Paint/Draw and Multimedia by:
- **resizing graphic elements**
- **copying/duplicating graphic elements**
- **using line properties--thickness, color, etc.**
- **using fill patterns/colors/shading**
- **adding sounds to multimedia file**

Grade 5. Through planned learning activities the student:

understands the concept of "audience"

creates presentations exhibiting synthesis of information which:
- **uses simple cause and effect**
- uses information appropriate to the task and the audience
- organizes ideas and information logically, e.g., time sequence

presents a solution to a problem using:
- simple oral and written reports
- **drawings, illustrations, and graphs**
- computer-generated drawings, illustrations, and graphs which are labeled to summarize findings
- constructions such as models or displays
- **dramatic, audio and video presentations**

using modeled examples, extends the use of Paint/Draw and Multimedia by:
- copying/duplicating and resizing graphic elements
- using line properties—thickness, color, etc.
- using fill patterns/colors/shading
- **beginning to construct multimedia presentations, adding video and sound**

Grade 6. Through planned learning activities the student:

understands the concept of "audience"

presents a solution to a problem using modeled examples which:

    demonstrate understanding and simple interpretations of information

    present ideas and information logically , e.g., time order, simple cause and effect

    make simple generalizations and draw simple conclusions

    use information appropriate to the task and the audience

    create written and oral reports, graphic, pictorial and dramatic presentations of similar complexity using modeled examples

    create presentations exhibiting synthesis of information

consolidates the use of Paint/Draw and Multimedia by:

    selecting multiple objects

    flipping/inverting and rotating objects

    creating text boxes/frames

    aligning graphic objects

    layering objects (move to front, back, etc.)

    creating simple multimedia presentations, including sound, video and graphics

develops skills in desktop publishing (graphics—borders, WordArt, clip art)

begins to construct multimedia presentations using modeled examples

Information Literacy Planning Organizer K–6
Overview of Evaluating Stage

Kindergarten. Through analysis of outcomes-based criteria the student:
respects the rights and opinions of others
develops concept of peer evaluation by giving and receiving feedback
shares this information with parents

Grade 1. Through analysis of outcomes-based criteria the student:
respects the rights and opinions of others
reflects on how well he or she worked through the process
develops concept of peer evaluation by giving and receiving feedback
shares this information with parents

Grade 2. Through analysis of outcomes-based criteria the student:
respects the rights and opinions of others
assesses own involvement with the topic or problem
identifies which skills are needed to make the task easier next time
reflects on how well he or she worked through the process
develops concept of peer evaluation by giving and receiving feedback
shares this information with parents

Grade 3. Through analysis of outcomes-based criteria the student:
respects the rights and opinions of others
assesses own involvement with the topic or problem
identifies which skills are needed to make the task easier next time
reflects on how well he or she worked through the process
develops concept of peer evaluation by giving and receiving feedback
discusses the appropriateness of the presentation in relationship to the original task
shares this information with parents

Grade 4. Through analysis of outcomes-based criteria the student:
acknowledges personal and group achievements
respects the rights and opinions of others
considers the quality, quantity and relevance of information
assesses own involvement with the topic or problem
identifies which skills are needed to make the task easier next time
identifies questions and issues arising from decisions and actions
assesses how well he or she worked through the process
responds constructively to assessment by teachers
develops concept of peer evaluation by giving and receiving feedback
uses a variety of evaluative strategies using modeled examples to assess and review learning strengths and
**   weaknesses, e.g., learning logs, reflective journals**
evaluates understanding and implementation of the set task criteria using modeled examples

Information Literacy Planning Organizer K–6
Overview of Evaluating Stage

Grade 5. Through analysis of outcomes-based criteria the student:

respects the rights and opinions of others

considers the quantity, quality and relevance of information

assesses own involvement with the task or problem

reflects on and evaluates the effectiveness of process used

evaluates personal ideas, feelings and actions and those of others

identifies questions and issues arising from decisions and actions

responds constructively to assessment by teachers

develops concept of peer evaluation by giving and receiving feedback

uses a variety of evaluative strategies using modeled examples to assess and review learning strengths and
   weaknesses, e.g., learning logs, reflective journals

evaluates understanding and implementation of the set task criteria using modeled examples

acknowledges personal and group achievements

Grade 6. Through analysis of outcomes-based criteria the student:

respects the rights and opinions of others

considers the quantity, quality and relevance of information

assesses own involvement with the topic or problem

reflects on and evaluates effectiveness of process used

evaluates personal ideas, feelings and actions and those of others

identifies questions and issues arising from decisions and actions

responds constructively to assessment by teachers

develops concept of peer evaluation by giving and receiving feedback

uses a variety of evaluative strategies using modeled examples to assess and review learning strengths and
   weaknesses, e.g., learning logs, reflective journals

evaluates understanding and implementation of the set task criteria using modeled examples

acknowledges personal and group achievements

Planning Organizers

Part 1, "Process Overviews," provided a list of the stages and skills of the information literacy process across grade levels to show the sequential and developmental nature of the process. The planning organizers in part 2 pull together by grade level the list of skills given in the process overviews in part 1. In addition to the six stages of the information process (defining, locating, selecting/analyzing, organizing/ synthesizing, creating/presenting, and evaluating), grades K–2 planning organizers include orienting skills. These skills pertain to the general physical layout of the school and an awareness of significant school personnel. Other orienting skills refer to responsible behavior toward property and people.

At the beginning of each year, supply teachers with a copy of the planning organizer for their grade levels. They list the names of the units (or themes or topics) they will teach at the top of the first page of the planning organizer *and* in the vertical columns above the skills listings.

Next, working collaboratively, the teacher and the library media specialist decide which skills will be appropriate for each unit. They record their decisions by placing a check mark in the corresponding skill rows under that unit heading. Then they plan the learning activities, resources, and assessment tasks that relate to the selected skills for a unit. (Many activities to use when teaching selected skills in the information literacy program may be found in part 3 of this book.) The teacher and library media specialist also determine who will take responsibility for various activities, and they plan the instructional groups and spaces they will use. For example, a particular activity might be presented by the library media specialist to a small group in the library. Spaces or resources that require scheduling can be tentatively reserved at this time as well.

If collaborative planning and teaching of information literacy skills are not an option, the planning organizers may be used effectively by either teachers or library media specialists as a guide to the sequential development of skills and planned lessons. Teachers of students with special needs should have a full set of the K–6 planning organizers to facilitate their planning.

At the end of each school year, place the planning organizers in a central location as part of an ongoing validation process to ensure that there is a whole-school approach to information literacy. Encourage teachers to refer to them when planning for the following school year.

As an alternative to using the planning organizers, this activity could be completed by opening the two Excel files and copying the appropriate skills from the process overview file on the CD-ROM to create a planning organizer by grade level. Then the specific skills for each unit could be copied to a second file and printed and stored as a record for the unit.

Kindergarten Planning Organizer

Class Teacher/s:		Class:		Year:

Unit:	Date:
Unit:	Date:
Unit:	Date:
Unit:	Date:
Unit:	Date:
Unit:	Date:
Unit:	Date:
Unit:	Date:

Units

ORIENTING. Through planned activities the student:

- knows location of kindergarten and library
- knows kindergarten, library, administration and other relevant personnel
- understands how to care for and organize own belongings
- respects property of others, including items on loan from school and libraries
- demonstrates care and respect in the use of equipment including computers

INFORMATION PROCESS

DEFINING. Through planned learning activities the student:

- discusses a given topic in response to an audio and/or visual stimulus
- draws on prior knowledge to brainstorm ideas and vocabulary for a given question
- understands and uses terminology: title, author, illustrator, spine, spine label

Kindergarten Planning Organizer

Units

LOCATING. Through planned learning activities the student:

- is aware of layout of kindergarten and library
- knows location of easy fiction and type of books housed there
- understands easy fiction resources are housed in a particular order
- learns borrowing procedures of school resources
- uses software icon menu on desktop
- uses keyboard--use of mouse and cursor (point and double clicking), Enter/Return key, locate and click, mouse pad, monitor
- interacts with story using mouse
- is aware of the Internet as a resource, especially e-mail

SELECTING/ANALYZING. Through planned learning activities the student:

- uses pictures, objects, live specimens, etc., to extract information
- selects books appropriate to interest using browsing techniques
- responds to teacher-led discussion relating to pictures, objects, live specimens, etc.
- interacts with resources through:
  - following directions
  - listening, observing and viewing
  - identifying a sequence of ideas
  - listening to and retelling stories in correct sequence
- makes selections using simple scanning techniques involving cover and illustrations
- makes simple decisions and justifies actions

Kindergarten Planning Organizer

	Units				

ORGANIZING/SYNTHESIZING. Through planned learning activities the student:

- organizes oral/pictorial information in sequence
- participates in teacher-led discussion
- sorts objects according to different characteristics
- begins to identify patterns and relationships using modeled examples
- begins to think independently
- begins to interact with peers in a fair manner
- verifies results of experiments using modeled examples
- practices hand and finger placement on keyboard
- interacts with a variety of educational software
- shares information with other children and adults

CREATING/PRESENTING. Through planned learning activities the student:

- presents information in simple oral and visual sequence
- presents a solution to a problem using a range of media, including:
  - picture sequence, collage, mural, model and computer drawing
  - dramatic presentations
- enacts role play/puppet presentations
- creates a response to a task with assistance which uses information selected for the purpose

EVALUATING. Through analysis of outcomes-based criteria the student:

- respects the rights and opinions of others
- develops concept of peer evaluation by giving and receiving feedback
- shares this information with parents

Grade 1 Planning Organizer

Class Teacher/s:	Class:	Year:

		Units
Unit:	Date:	
Unit:	Date:	
Unit:	Date:	
Unit:	Date:	
Unit:	Date:	
Unit:	Date:	
Unit:	Date:	
Unit:	Date:	

ORIENTING. Through planned activities the student:

- knows location of all relevant areas of school
- knows classroom, library, administration and other relevant personnel
- understands how to care for and organize own belongings
- respects property of others, including items on loan from school and libraries
- understands rules for hardware, software use
- demonstrates care in the use of equipment
- demonstrates care and respect in the use of equipment including computers

INFORMATION PROCESS

DEFINING. Through planned learning activities the student:

- discusses a given topic in response to an audio and/or visual stimulus
- draws on prior knowledge to brainstorm ideas and vocabulary for a given question
- categorizes information into lists (written or graphic)
- brainstorms possible sources of new information
- understands and uses terminology: title, author, illustrator, spine, spine label

LOCATING. Through planned learning activities the student:

- is aware of layout of classroom, library and school
- knows location of easy fiction and type of books found there

Grade 1 Planning Organizer

LOCATING [cont]. Through planned learning activities the student:

is aware that easy fiction is shelved in alphabetical order according to last name of author											
learns borrowing procedures for school resources											
differentiates between fiction and nonfiction resources and their location											
is aware of primary resources as a source of information, e.g., first-hand experience, people, concrete objects											
is aware of secondary resources as a source of information, e.g., book, pictures, AV materials											
is aware of computer system skills using modeled examples:											
can turn computer on											
uses terminology--monitor, keyboard, mouse, disk drive, printer, disk, CD-ROM											
understands and uses keyboard--space bar, Enter/Return, caps lock											
interacts with story using mouse											
practices hand and finger placement on keyboard											
uses file menu to exit program											
is aware of the Internet and e-mail as a communication tool and information source											

SELECTING/ANALYZING. Through planned learning activities the student:

selects books appropriate to interest and reading ability using browsing techniques											
gains information through discussion using pictures, objects, live specimens, etc.											
interacts with resources through:											
following directions											
listening, observing and viewing in response to focus questions											
identifying the main idea and key words											
identifying a sequence of ideas											
distinguishing between narrative and information texts											
listening to and retelling stories in correct sequence											
makes selections using simple scanning techniques involving cover, title and illustrations											
makes simple decisions and justifies actions											
records relevant information using modeled examples by arranging ideas, events, and facts in sequence											
from oral, pictorial, and written sources											
constructs sentences orally using identified key words											
is aware of people with special knowledge as a primary resource											

ORGANIZING/SYNTHESIZING. Through planned learning activities the student:

organizes oral/pictorial/written information in sequence											
participates in teacher-led discussion to categorize information											

Grade 1 Planning Organizer

ORGANIZING/SYNTHESIZING [cont]. Through planned learning activities the student:

- sorts objects according to different characteristics
- **identifies patterns and relationships using modeled examples**
- **begins to think independently**
- **interacts with peers in a fair manner**
- **participates in group discussion to propose a solution to a problem**
- verifies results of experiments using modeled examples
- **categorizes information into list format, both written and graphic**
- **is introduced to the use of simple word processing through:**
  - an awareness of letters on keyboard if interested and ready
  - opening word processing application
  - entering text, e.g., own name
  - printing document
  - an awareness of delete/backspace key
- interacts with a variety of educational software
- **decides on an appropriate presentation format using modeled examples**

CREATING/PRESENTING. Through planned learning activities the student:

- **presents information in oral, written, and visual sequence**
- presents a solution to a problem using a range of media, including:
  - picture sequence, collage, mural, model, and computer drawing
  - dramatic presentations
- **begins to use Paint/Draw on computer with guidance:**
  - freehand drawing--pencil
  - shape tools--box, circle
  - **selects objects with selection tool**
  - **deletes selected objects**
- enacts role play/puppet presentations
- **creates a response to a task/topic which uses information selected for the purpose**
- **presents word processed document containing student's name and a sentence of text, printed with assistance**

EVALUATING. Through analysis of outcomes-based criteria the student:

- respects the rights and opinions of others
- **reflects on how well he or she worked through the process**
- develops concept of peer evaluation by giving and receiving feedback
- shares this information with parents

Grade 2 Planning Organizer

Class: **Year:**

Class Teacher/s:

Unit: Date:

Unit: Date:

Unit: Date:

Unit: Date:

Unit: Date:

Unit: Date:

Unit: Date:

Unit: Date:

Units

ORIENTING. Through planned activities the student:

understands how to care for and organize own belongings

respects property of others, including items on loan from school and libraries

learns borrowing procedures for classroom resources

understands rules for computer hardware and software use

demonstrates care in the use of equipment including computers

INFORMATION PROCESS

DEFINING. Through planned learning activities the student:

discusses a given topic in response to an audio and/or visual stimulus

draws on prior knowledge to brainstorm key ideas and vocabulary for a given question

uses key ideas to formulate focus questions using teacher-modeled examples

categorizes information into lists (written or graphic)

brainstorms possible sources of new information

understands and uses terminology: title, author, illustrator, spine, spine label

LOCATING. Through planned learning activities the student:

is aware of layout of library and school

differentiates between fiction and nonfiction sections of the library and uses the spine label to identify resources

is aware that nonfiction resources are shelved in numerical order

finds resources in both school library and public libraries with assistance

Grade 2 Planning Organizer

LOCATING [cont]. Through planned learning activities the student:

is aware of primary resources as a source of information, e.g., first-hand experience, people, concrete objects

is aware of secondary resources as a source of information, e.g., book, pictures, AV materials, magazines

begins to use contents and index pages of nonfiction books using key words

is aware of computer system skills through modeled examples:

by saving into appropriate folders/directories

by retrieving saved document

by being able to turn computer on/off correctly

understands and uses keyboard–space bar, Enter/Return, mouse, cursor, locate and click, caps lock

is aware of finger placement on keyboard home keys

by using file menu to exit program

acquires information from different instructional displays

is aware of search strategies to help select and locate resources

is aware of the Internet (e-mail) as a communication tool and information source

SELECTING/ANALYZING. Through planned learning activities the student:

selects books appropriate to interest and reading ability using browsing techniques

gains information through discussion using pictures, objects, live specimens, etc.

compares different preselected resources on a topic deciding which is appropriate

makes selections using simple scanning techniques involving cover, title and illustrations

interacts with the resources through:

following directions

listening, observing and viewing in response to focus questions

identifying the main idea and key words

identifying a sequence of ideas

distinguishing between narrative and information texts

listening to and retelling stories in correct sequence

asks questions appropriately using modeled examples

records relevant information using modeled examples by:

listing key words under main ideas

arranging ideas, events and facts in sequence from oral, pictorial and written sources

constructs sentences orally using identified key words

is aware of people with special knowledge as a primary resource

Grade 2 Planning Organizer

ORGANIZING/SYNTHESIZING. Through planned learning activities the student:

- participates in teacher-led discussion to categorize information
- identifies patterns and relationships with guidance
- recognizes the need for tolerance and respect for the opinions of peers
- participates in group discussion to propose a solution to a problem
- understands that ideas are more readily accepted if supported by sound reasoning
- verifies results of experiments using modeled examples
- categorizes information into list format, both written and graphic
- using modeled examples, extends the use of word processing by:
  - entering text--highlight, edit
  - changing text--font/color, bold/italic/underline
  - resizing text
  - changing text alignment
- has an awareness of letters on keyboard
- decides on an appropriate presentation format using modeled examples

CREATING/PRESENTING. Through planned learning activities the student:

- begins to understand the concept of "audience"
- creates presentations exhibiting synthesis of information which:
  - uses information appropriate to the task and the audience
  - presents information in oral, written, and visual sequence
  - presents a solution to a problem using a range of media, including:
    - picture sequence, collage, mural, model, and computer drawing
    - dramatic presentations
- uses Paint/Draw on computer with guidance including:
  - drawing straight lines
  - using eraser
  - using shape tools
  - using paintbrush/fill
- presents word-processed document containing student's name and a paragraph of text, printed with assistance

EVALUATING. Through analysis of outcomes-based criteria the student:

- respects the rights and opinions of others
- assesses own involvement with the topic or problem
- identifies which skills are needed to make the task easier next time
- reflects on how well he or she worked through the process
- develops concept of peer evaluation by giving and receiving feedback
- shares this information with parents

Grade 3 Planning Organizer

Class Teacher/s:	Class:	Year:
Unit:	Date:	
Unit:	Date:	
Unit:	Date:	
Unit:	Date:	
Unit:	Date:	
Unit:	Date:	
Unit:	Date:	
	Units	

INFORMATION PROCESS

DEFINING. Through planned learning activities the student:

- discusses a given topic in response to an audio and/or visual stimulus
- draws on prior knowledge to brainstorm key ideas and vocabulary for a topic
- **understands the organizing principle of main heading**
- **devises focus questions in groups using modeled examples**
- **organizes focus questions into headings from clustered ideas using modeled examples**
- **contributes to a teacher-devised search plan which lists:**
  - **headings**
  - **key words and possible search terms**
  - **focus questions**
- likely sources of information
- understands and uses terminology: publisher, series, contents, index

Grade 3 Planning Organizer

LOCATING. Through planned learning activities the student:

is aware of layout of library and school																
differentiates between fiction and nonfiction sections of the library and uses the spine label to identify resources																
is aware that nonfiction resources are shelved in numerical order																
finds resources in both school library and public libraries with assistance																
follows a search plan with assistance																
locates fiction using spine label																
locates nonfiction using Dewey decimal classification system																
locates appropriate resources in both school library and public libraries with assistance																
begins to use contents and index pages of nonfiction books using key words																
begins to identify primary and secondary sources of information																
uses a range of resources as sources of information, e.g., encyclopedias, videos, CD-ROM																
is aware of author, title or subject access to resources																
is aware of key word searches using CD-ROM and online technology																
using modeled examples, is aware of Internet/e-mail through:																
being aware of e-mail communication																
locating bookmarked Internet sites with assistance																
participating in online projects to locate, contribute, and gather information																
starting browser software																
using back/forward navigation arrows in browser																
identifying and using links on a Web page																
is aware of computer system skills using modeled examples by:																
saving into appropriate folders/directories																
retrieving saved document																
being able to turn computer on/off correctly																
reading and using software text and icon menu																
locating, reading and responding to software instructions																
interacting with story using mouse																
understands the purpose of displays and directional signage																
locates and borrows magazines with assistance																

Grade 3 Planning Organizer

SELECTING/ANALYZING. Through planned learning activities the student:

selects books appropriate to interest and reading ability using browsing techniques

gains information through discussion using pictures, objects, live specimens, etc.

compares different preselected resources on a topic deciding which is appropriate

makes selections using simple scanning techniques involving cover, title and illustrations

interacts with the resources through:

listening, observing and viewing in response to focus questions

identifying the main idea and key words

identifying a sequence of ideas

distinguishing between narrative and information texts

listening to and retelling stories in correct sequence

asks questions appropriately with guidance

records relevant information using modeled examples by:

listing key words under main ideas

arranging ideas, events and facts in sequence from oral, pictorial and written sources

writing sentences using identified key words

is aware of people with special knowledge as a primary resource

ORGANIZING/SYNTHESIZING. Through planned learning activities the student:

synthesizes selected information connecting similar ideas

recognizes the need for tolerance and respect for the opinions of peers

participates in group discussion to propose a solution to a problem

understands that ideas are more readily accepted if supported by sound reasoning

verifies results of experiments using modeled examples

categorizes information into list format

makes notes using modeled techniques, e.g., written bulleted points, note-taking template

using modeled examples, extends the use of word processing by:

entering and editing text

justifying text

changing text--font/color, bold/italic/underline

resizing text

changing text alignment

highlighting text

saving

printing

Grade 3 Planning Organizer

ORGANIZING/SYNTHESIZING [cont]. Through planned learning activities the student:

using modeled examples, extends the use of word processing by:

using line spacing

extends knowledge of finger placement on keyboard using both hands (left side, right side)

using modeled examples, is introduced to databases through:

opening, browsing and searching a commercial database, e.g., encyclopedia

decides on an appropriate presentation format using modeled examples

CREATING/PRESENTING. Through planned learning activities the student:

begins to understand the concept of "audience"

creates presentations exhibiting synthesis of information which:

uses information appropriate to the task and the audience

organizes ideas and information logically, e.g., time sequence

presents a solution to a problem using:

simple oral and written descriptions

drawings

constructions such as models or displays

dramatic presentations

selectively prints presentations, e.g., word-processed paragraph

uses Paint/Draw with guidance including:

drawing straight lines

using eraser

using shape tools

using paintbrush/fill

EVALUATING. Through analysis of outcomes-based criteria the student:

respects the rights and opinions of others

assesses own involvement with the topic or problem

identifies which skills are needed to make the task easier next time

reflects on how well he or she worked through the process

develops concept of peer evaluation by giving and receiving feedback

discusses the appropriateness of the presentation in relationship to the original task

shares this information with parents

Grade 4 Planning Organizer

Class Teacher/s:	Class:	Year:

Unit:	Date:	
Unit:	Date:	
Unit:	Date:	
Unit:	Date:	
Unit:	Date:	
Unit:	Date:	
Unit:	Date:	
Unit:	Date:	

Units

INFORMATION PROCESS

DEFINING. Through planned learning activities the student:

- draws on prior knowledge to brainstorm key ideas and vocabulary for a topic
- **devises focus questions in groups and individually using modeled examples**
- **organizes focus questions into headings from clustered ideas with guidance**
- contributes to a teacher-devised search plan which lists:
  - headings
  - key words and possible search terms
  - focus questions
  - likely sources of information

LOCATING. Through planned learning activities the student:

- follows a search plan with assistance
- locates fiction using spine label
- **locates reference materials**
- **uses reference tools--atlas, telephone book, encyclopedia, thesaurus, dictionary, reference CD-ROM**
- **uses author, title, subject access in search strategy to identify the shelf label of a resource**
- using modeled examples, is aware of Internet/e-mail through:
- **using e-mail as a form of communication and possible source of information**
- locating bookmarked Internet sites with assistance
- participating in online projects to locate, contribute and gather information

Grade 4 Planning Organizer

LOCATING [cont]. Through planned learning activities the student:

using back/forward navigation arrows in browser															
is aware of computer system skills using modeled examples by:															
saving into appropriate folders/directories															
retrieving saved document															
using Save and Save as appropriately															
minimizing open documents/programs															
identifies primary and secondary sources of information															
locates appropriate resources using the Dewey decimal classification system															
selects materials by scanning table of contents, assessing readability, presentation and quality of illustrations															
borrows magazines with assistance															
is aware of key word searches using CD-ROM and online technology															
locates reference materials, magazines, nonfiction, software, bookmarked Internet sites															
uses reference books (encyclopedia, telephone directory) to locate information															
uses author, title, subject, series to access resources through search strategies															
identifies primary and secondary sources of information															
gathers data from simple interviews, excursions, surveys, questionnaires															
prejudges the relative worth of resources in terms of purpose															
is aware of Internet search engines as a source of information															
uses given Internet addresses with assistance															

SELECTING/ANALYZING. Through planned learning activities the student:

evaluates appropriateness of resources using modeled examples															
uses appropriate note-taking templates using modeled examples															
identifies and records relevant information from a resource by:															
using a note-making strategy, e.g., listing															
clustering notes under subheadings															
uses focus questions to identify key information and ideas from print and non-print sources															
compares information from different sources using modeled techniques															
records bibliographic sources of information using author, title, publisher, date using modeled examples															
is aware of a variety of primary and secondary sources using modeled examples															

Grade 4 Planning Organizer

ORGANIZING/SYNTHESIZING. Through planned learning activities the student:

synthesizes selected information connecting similar ideas

participates in group discussion to propose a solution to a problem

verifies results of experiments using modeled examples

categorizes information according to a framework of headings using modeled examples

makes notes using modeled techniques, e.g., written bulleted points, note-taking template

using modeled examples, extends the use of word processing by:

entering and editing text

making notes using word processor or other software

using Tab function

understanding the difference between Cut and Copy

copying selected text

cutting and pasting text

changes font size--before and after entering text

practices posture and keyboard drills, e.g., hand and finger placement

using modeled examples, is introduced to databases through:

opening, browsing and searching a commercial database, e.g., encyclopedia

using modeled examples, is introduced to the use of spreadsheets by:

opening a prepared spreadsheet

entering data into specific cells

decides on an appropriate presentation format using modeled examples

CREATING/PRESENTING. Through planned learning activities the student:

understands the concept of "audience"

creates presentations exhibiting synthesis of information which:

uses logical structures such as time sequences, grids

uses information appropriate to the task and the audience

presents a solution to a problem using:

simple oral and written reports

drawings, illustrations and simple bar graphs

computer-generated drawings, illustrations, and simple bar graphs which are labeled to summarize findings

constructions such as models or displays

dramatic presentations

simple audio presentations

Grade 4 Planning Organizer

CREATING/PRESENTING [cont]. Through planned learning activities the student:

using modeled examples, extends the use of Paint/Draw and Multimedia by:

resizing graphic elements											
copying/duplicating graphic elements											
using line properties--thickness, color, etc.											
using fill patterns/colors/shading											
adding sounds to multimedia file											

EVALUATING. Through analysis of outcomes-based criteria the student:

acknowledges personal and group achievements											
respects the rights and opinions of others											
considers the quality, quantity and relevance of information											
assesses own involvement with the topic or problem											
identifies which skills are needed to make the task easier next time											
identifies questions and issues arising from decisions and actions											
assesses how well he or she worked through the process											
responds constructively to assessment by teachers											
develops concept of peer evaluation by giving and receiving feedback											
uses a variety of evaluative strategies using modeled examples to assess and review learning strengths and weaknesses,											
e.g., learning logs, reflective journals											
evaluates understanding and implementation of the set task criteria using modeled examples											

Grade 5 Planning Organizer

Class: **Year:**

Class Teacher/s:

Unit:	Date:
Unit:	Date:
Unit:	Date:
Unit:	Date:
Unit:	Date:
Unit:	Date:
Unit:	Date:
Unit:	Date:

Units

INFORMATION PROCESS

DEFINING. Through planned learning activities the student:
- draws on prior knowledge to brainstorm and cluster ideas with teachers and peers
- analyzes and clarifies a given task using modeled techniques
- devises focus questions in groups and individually using modeled examples
- organizes focus questions into headings from clustered ideas with guidance
- prepares a group search plan which lists:
  - headings
  - key words and possible search terms
  - focus questions
  - likely sources of information

LOCATING. Through planned learning activities the student:
- follows a search plan adding relevant information
- locates reference materials, magazines, nonfiction, software, bookmarked Internet sites
- uses reference books (encyclopedia, telephone directory) to locate information
- uses author, title, subject, series to access resources

Grade 5 Planning Organizer

LOCATING [cont]. Through planned learning activities the student:

using modeled examples extends use of Internet/e-mail by:

using given Internet addresses with assistance

bookmarking a location

composing and sending e-mail

accessing and reading e-mail

replying to an e-mail message

forwarding an e-mail message

copying/pasting from Web page to document

being aware of Internet search engines as a source of information

is aware of computer system skills using modeled examples by:

saving into appropriate folders/directories

retrieving saved document

using Save and Save as appropriately

minimizing open documents/programs

identifies primary and secondary sources of information

locates appropriate resources using the Dewey decimal classification system

gathers data from simple interviews, field trips, surveys, questionnaires

prejudges the relative worth of resources in terms of purpose

is aware of periodical indexes

SELECTING/ANALYZING. Through planned learning activities the student:

selects resources using modeled techniques by:

skimming and scanning

using contents, index and text headings

using key words and key phrases

evaluates appropriateness of resources using modeled examples

modifies focus questions using modeled techniques

uses appropriate note-taking templates using modeled examples

identifies and records relevant information from a resource

records information using modeled examples by:

using a note-taking strategy, e.g., concept mapping, outlining, list making

clustering notes under subheadings

makes simple comparisons between the purpose of different writing styles using modeled examples

analyzes consequences of group or community decision using modeled examples

Grade 5 Planning Organizer

SELECTING/ANALYZING [cont]. Through planned learning activities the student:

compares information from different sources using modeled techniques							
recognizes when a statement is a generalization							
records bibliographic sources of information using author, title, publisher, date, http, date of download using modeled examples							
uses a variety of primary and secondary sources using modeled examples							

ORGANIZING/SYNTHESIZING. Through planned learning activities the student:

synthesizes selected information connecting similar ideas and begins to predict possible outcomes							
is aware there may be alternative solutions to a problem							
uses information from various resources to support an argument							
based on prior knowledge and new information, proposes a solution through group discussion to a set problem which:							
organizes ideas and information logically							
makes simple generalizations and draws simple conclusions							
verifies results of experiments using modeled examples							
categorizes information according to a framework of headings using modeled examples							
makes notes using modeled techniques, e.g., written bulleted points, note-taking template, clipboards, etc.							
using modeled examples, extends the use of word processing by:							
making notes using word processor or other software							
making notes directly from screen							
practicing keyboard drills, e.g., hand and finger placement							
using spell checker							
using columns							
changing page orientation (landscape/portrait)							
changing size of page, e.g., 75% view							
inserting graphics							
manipulating graphics, e.g., resizing							
using modeled examples, is introduced to databases through:							
opening, browsing and searching a commercial database, e.g., encyclopedia							
using modeled examples, is introduced to the use of spreadsheets by:							
opening a prepared spreadsheet							
entering data into specific cells							
recognizes information deficiencies							
demonstrates sound reasoning when challenged							
decides on an appropriate presentation format using modeled examples							

Grade 5 Planning Organizer

CREATING/PRESENTING. Through planned learning activities the student:

- understands the concept of "audience"
- creates presentations exhibiting synthesis of information which:
- **uses simple cause and effect**
  - uses information appropriate to the task and the audience
  - organizes ideas and information logically, e.g., time sequence
- presents a solution to a problem using:
  - simple oral and written reports
  - drawings, illustrations, and graphs
  - computer-generated drawings, illustrations and graphs which are labeled to summarize findings
  - constructions such as models or displays
- **dramatic, audio and video presentations**
- using modeled examples, extends the use of Paint/Draw and Multimedia by:
  - copying/duplicating, and resizing graphic elements
  - using line properties--thickness, color, etc.
  - using fill patterns/colors/shading
- **beginning to construct multimedia presentations, adding video and sound**

EVALUATING. Through analysis of outcomes-based criteria the student:

- respects the rights and opinions of others
- considers the quantity, quality and relevance of information
- assesses own involvement with the task or problem
- **reflects on and evaluates the effectiveness of process used**
- **evaluates personal ideas, feelings and actions and those of others**
- identifies questions and issues arising from decisions and actions
- responds constructively to assessment by teachers
- develops concept of peer evaluation by giving and receiving feedback
- uses a variety of evaluative strategies using modeled examples to assess and review learning strengths and weaknesses, e.g., learning logs, reflective journals
- evaluates understanding and implementation of the set task criteria using modeled examples
- **acknowledges personal and group achievements**

Grade 6 Planning Organizer

Class Teacher/s:	Class:	Year:

Unit:	Date:
Unit:	Date:
Unit:	Date:
Unit:	Date:
Unit:	Date:
Unit:	Date:
Unit:	Date:
Unit:	Date:

Units

INFORMATION PROCESS

DEFINING. Through planned learning activities the student:

- develops appropriate questioning techniques through extensive modeling to clarify requirements of task
- analyzes and clarifies a given task with guidance
- selects from a range of topics using modeled techniques
- draws on prior knowledge to brainstorm and cluster ideas with guidance
- identifies and interprets key words in task using modeled techniques
- develops focus questions using modeled techniques
- prepares a simple search plan which lists:
- headings and subheadings
- key words and possible search terms
- focus questions
- likely sources of information

LOCATING. Through planned learning activities the student:

- follows a search plan using key words and related terms, modifying where necessary
- determines the type of resource most appropriate for the topic
- identifies and locates book and nonbook resources including:
- understanding organization of resources in school and local libraries
- recognizing the value of fiction for specific topics, e.g., historical fiction
- becoming familiar with limited number of appropriate search engines using modeled techniques

Grade 6 Planning Organizer

LOCATING [cont]. Through planned learning activities the student:

using simple and combined terms to search catalog, Internet and CD-ROM sources							
choosing broader or narrower terms to refine search results							
using Help function to locate information and refine searches							
searching for information using given Internet addresses							
using information from the wider community							
accesses periodical indexes using modeled techniques							
identifies appropriate resources by:							
using skimming and scanning techniques to survey readability in electronic and print resources							
using contents, index and text headings for all types of resources							
with assistance, recognizes the differences in purpose and coverage of:							
magazines, newspaper, pamphlets, film, special reference materials, CD-ROM, Web searches, e-mail							
recognizes where currency of information is necessary							
recognizes the need to locate a variety of resources representing a range of views							
with guidance, extends use of Internet/e-mail by:							
using given Internet addresses with assistance							
bookmarking a location							
composing and sending e-mail							
accessing and reading e-mail							
forwarding and replying to an e-mail message							
copying/pasting from Web page to document							
being aware of Internet search engines as a source of information							
being aware of Web page structure							
extends use of computer system skills using modeled examples by:							
deleting, copying and moving files							
identifies and locates information from both primary and secondary sources using modeled techniques							
uses special print and non-print reference resources using modeled examples							
uses index and knowledge of newspaper structure to select appropriate articles							
uses key words, volume, index and cross-references to find information in print and non-print encyclopedias							
uses range of equipment to access information, e.g., telephone, fax, computer, scanner, digital camera using modeled techniques							
uses e-mail to discuss topics and to facilitate cooperative activities using modeled examples							
loads software for information retrieval							

SELECTING/ANALYZING. Through planned learning activities the student:

selects resources using modeled techniques by:							
skimming and scanning							

Grade 6 Planning Organizer

SELECTING/ANALYZING [cont]. Through planned learning activities the student:

- using contents, index, text headings, key words, and key phrases
- evaluates appropriateness of resources using modeled examples
- modifies focus questions using modeled techniques
- **devises appropriate note-taking templates using modeled examples**
- records information using modeled examples by:
- using a note-taking strategy, e.g., concept mapping, outline, list making
- clustering notes under subheadings
- **selecting appropriate graphic organizer**
- **understands that different accounts of the same event may vary**
- makes simple comparisons between the purpose of different writing styles using modeled examples
- **analyzes consequences of group or community decision**
- compares information from different sources using modeled techniques
- **is aware of the need for adequate data before drawing conclusions**
- records bibliographic sources of information using author, title, publisher, date, http, date of download using modeled examples
- **understands and complies with copyright requirements using modeled examples**
- **observes netiquette conventions when communicating electronically using modeled techniques**
- **understands there may be various interpretations of data**
- uses a variety of primary and secondary sources using modeled examples

ORGANIZING/SYNTHESIZING. Through planned learning activities the student:

- **using modeled examples, begins to discriminate between fact and opinion**
- synthesizes selected information connecting similar ideas and begins to predict possible outcomes
- is aware there may be alternative solutions to a problem
- uses information from various resources to support an argument
- **understands that comparisons must be based on similar characteristics**
- **recognizes there may be various interpretations of data**
- **engages in reflective thinking to analyze and clarify a problem**
- **engages in group discussion to analyze and clarify a problem**
- **proposes a solution to a set problem based on prior knowledge and new information which:**
- organize ideas and information logically
- make simple generalizations and draw simple conclusions
- verifies results of experiments using modeled examples
- categorizes information according to a framework of headings and subheadings using modeled examples

Grade 6 Planning Organizer

ORGANIZING/SYNTHESIZING [cont]. Through planned learning activities the student:

selectively cuts and pastes information from an electronic source with guidance												
to quote a source												
to make notes												
makes notes using modeled techniques, e.g., written bulleted points, note-taking template, clipboards, etc.												
consolidates the use of word processing skills by:												
selectively cutting and pasting information from an electronic source with guidance												
making notes using word processor or other software												
making notes directly from screen												
using keyboard drills, Spelling, Grammar Check, Undo, Select all, Page Setup												
using lists/bullets												
creating and inserting simple tables												
wrapping text around graphics												
formatting text appropriate to text type												
extends the use of databases using modeled examples through:												
browsing, editing and adding records in a class-created database												
sorting and deleting records												
using Find function to search for specific criteria												
extends the use of spreadsheets by:												
editing data in a prepared spreadsheet												
understanding the concept of a spreadsheet												
creating a new spreadsheet												
understanding the difference between columns and rows												
applying simple formulas--some digits (addition)												
formatting entries, e.g., bold												
recognizes information deficiencies and locates additional information using modeled examples												
understands the need for sound reasoning when challenged												
develops the ability to have faith in own judgment and point of view												
decides on an appropriate presentation format using modeled examples												
organizes ideas and information logically, e.g., time order, simple cause and effect												
presents information using appropriate organizational frameworks with assistance, e.g.,												
written and word-processed reports, recounts, procedures and lists												
using titles and subtitles appropriately												
oral reports, descriptions, and comparisons supported by graphic and pictorial information												
construction such as models and displays, diagrams and posters												
plays, role play												
desktop publishing (borders, WordArt, clip art)												
multimedia presentations using scanner, digital camera, video images and sound												

Grade 6 Planning Organizer

CREATING/PRESENTING. Through planned learning activities the student:

understands the concept of "audience"

presents a solution to a problem using modeled examples that:

demonstrate understanding and simple interpretations of information

present ideas and information logically, e.g., time order, simple cause and effect

make simple generalizations and draw simple conclusions

use information appropriate to the task and the audience

create written and oral reports, graphic, pictorial and dramatic presentations of similar complexity using modeled examples

create presentations exhibiting synthesis of information

consolidates the use of Paint/Draw and Multimedia by:

selecting multiple objects

flipping/inverting and rotating objects

creating text boxes/frames

aligning graphic objects

layering objects (move to front, back, etc.)

creating simple multimedia presentations, including sound, video and graphics

develops skills in desktop publishing (graphics--borders, WordArt, clip art)

begins to construct multimedia presentations using modeled examples

EVALUATING. Through analysis of outcomes-based criteria the student:

respects the rights and opinions of others

considers the quantity, quality and relevance of information

assesses own involvement with the topic or problem

reflects on and evaluates effectiveness of process used

evaluates personal ideas, feelings and actions and those of others

identifies questions and issues arising from decisions and actions

responds constructively to assessment by teachers

develops concept of peer evaluation by giving and receiving feedback

uses a variety of evaluative strategies using modeled examples to assess and review learning strengths and weaknesses, e.g., learning logs, reflective journals

evaluates understanding and implementation of the set task criteria using modeled examples

acknowledges personal and group achievements

3

Teaching Tools

The teaching tools are reproducible forms that support the teaching of information literacy skills across the curriculum. These teaching support worksheets and strategies complement the information literacy planning organizers developed in part 2.

The worksheets are designed to

- provide a comprehensive structure for teaching information literacy using the six-stage information literacy process—defining, locating, selecting/analyzing, organizing/synthesizing, creating/presenting, and evaluating

- provide a generic framework for use across the curriculum

- encourage students to develop a consistent approach to research tasks

- assist teachers with the teaching of information literacy skills (teaching tips for selected skills are included to stimulate teaching ideas)

- assist a wide range of teaching professionals including teachers of ESL, students with special needs, etc.

How to Use the Teaching Tools

As explained in part 2, teachers and library media specialists collaboratively plan units using the school-based information literacy planning organizers. After the relevant skills have been identified for inclusion in the unit, the planners decide on activities to develop these skills. Teachers and the library media specialist select from the teaching tools those activities that support the instruction of these skills according to the curriculum content of the unit and appropriate assessment tasks. The teaching tools contain activities based on a broad range of developmental levels and student competencies.

Student Competencies

To be prepared for the twenty-first century, students must have the competencies and skills to learn and think creatively, make informed decisions, and solve problems. They need to organize information and process symbols, acquire and apply new knowledge and skills, and make connections to relationships when solving a problem. The information literacy skills as set out in the planning organizers will assist students in acquiring these skills and in developing personal qualities. The personal qualities include those identified by the U.S. Secretary of Labor's Commission on Achieving Necessary Skills:

- *Responsibility*—exerts a high level of effort and perseveres toward goal attainment
- *Self-esteem*—believes in own self-worth and maintains a positive view of self
- *Sociability*—demonstrates understanding, friendliness, adaptability, empathy, and politeness in group settings
- *Self-management*—assesses self accurately, sets personal goals, monitors progress, and exhibits self-control
- *Integrity/honesty*—chooses ethical courses of action[1]

During the course of our daily lives we are constantly problem solving—making choices based on prior knowledge combined with new information to create new knowledge. To develop skills in problem solving and to overcome the problem of plagiarism, students must be given the opportunity to offer original solutions to a problem. Therefore, teachers are encouraged to frame a unit of work as a problem or task rather than as a topic so that students will create and present original ideas instead of simply reading and regurgitating the knowledge of others. Students are challenged and are frequently far more motivated by the prospect of solving a problem, particularly if the problem can be related to their own experiences or real-life situations. Many teachers have indicated that students often achieve outcomes far beyond expectations when offered a problem-solving task.

The following examples highlight the difference between defining a unit as a topic versus as a problem to be solved or a task to be accomplished:

Topic: Celebrations

Problem/Task: What do we need to do to prepare a birthday party for someone?

Topic: Native Animals

Problem/Task: If you were designing a zoo for native animals, which animals would you choose to show visitors to your country? Design an animal enclosure for one of these animals to show how it lives in its natural environment.

Problems or tasks call for active participation of students. When defining units in terms of a problem or task, teachers and library media specialists will want to use specific verbs, such as the following:

advertise	classify	construct	discuss
improve	devise	create	invent
investigate	use	predict	plan
build	identify	explain	separate
solve	show	illustrate	select
choose	decide	design	imagine
prepare			

Embedding Technology in the Information Process

The table on pages 53–54 is an example of how technology may be embedded in the information process. It includes a comparison between print-based or low-tech and high-tech approaches to problem solving or task completion. The high-tech examples use currently available software.

Using the Unit Planner

The unit planner (see page 52) pulls together plans for all aspects of a unit. Teachers and library media specialists can work together to complete a unit planner for each unit they include in their planning organizers (see part 2). They may start by defining the purpose of the unit as a problem or task and recording it at the top of the form. Then they can transfer the list of skills for that unit from their overall planning sheets created in part 2. Next, they can determine the activities that are appropriate for those skills, pulling from the teaching tools blackline masters and from activities of their own creation. They determine how they will assess whether students have mastered those skills or shown an adequate grasp of the process and record those criteria in the assessment column. Finally, using the embedding technology chart supplemented by their own knowledge of locally available resources, they record the high-tech or low-tech resources they plan to have students use in each stage of the information literacy process for solving the unit's problem or completing its task. By using this planning sheet, teachers and library media specialists have a complete overview of a unit that includes all aspects of the information literacy process.

NOTE

1. U.S. Dept. of Labor, Secretary's Commission on Achieving Necessary Skills (SCANS), *What Work Requires of Schools: A SCANS Report for America 2000* (Washington, D.C.: U.S. Dept. of Labor, 1991), xvii–xviii.

Unit Planner

Class teacher/s:	Class/group:	Commencing date:	Duration of unit:

Unit:

	Activities: (examples)	Assessment:	Resources: (focus only)
Defining:			
Locating:			
Selecting/Analyzing:			
Organizing/Synthesizing:			
Creating/Presenting:			
Evaluating:			

Embedding Technology in the Information Literacy Process

Problem setting

Task	Strategy	High-Tech Approach	Low-Tech Approach
Create a problem or meaningful context for the content	Use a community service project or a problem created by students or teacher that is relevant to the children's experiences	Use an Internet-based curriculum project as a context	Use the media or children's experiences

Defining the problem

KWL (K=what we know, W=what we want to know, L=what we need to learn) or concept map	Mind maps	Inspiration Claris Works Draw	Blackline master of a concept map
Outline	Outlining	Microsoft Word	Pencil and paper
SWOT (Strengths, Weaknesses, Opportunities, Threats) analysis	Recording	Inspiration Claris Works Word Processing Microsoft Word	Pencil and paper
Brainstorm	Share ideas	e-mail lists discussion boards	Class discussion Multiage projects teams Talk to family at home Cross-class discussions

Locating information

Locate resources	Books, videos, pictures	Automated library	Browsing the local library
Locate resources	CD-ROM searching	Encarta CD Groliers CD World Book CD	Print encyclopedias
Locate resources	Internet searching	AltaVista HotBot	No low-tech alternative
Locate resources	Internet indexes	Yahooligans	No low-tech alternative
Primary sources	E-mail interviews	Microsoft Express E-mail	Personal interviews
Data collection	Experiment	Remote sensing	Hands-on experiments

Embedding Technology in the Information Literacy Process

Selecting/Analyzing

Task	Strategy	High Tech	Low Tech
Recording facts and ideas	Outlining	Microsoft Word Claris Works Word 　Processing	Pencil and paper 3 X 5 cards
	Note taking	Microsoft Encarta 　Research Organizer World Book 　Homework Wizards	Pencil and paper

Organizing/Synthesizing

	Spreadsheet	Claris Works Spreadsheet Microsoft Excel	Y Chart X Chart
	Database	Claris Works Database Microsoft Access	Venn diagrams
	Outline	Claris Works Word 　Processing	Pencil and paper
	Note taking	World Book	Pencil and paper
	Time lines	Timeline Wizard	

Creating/Presenting

		Microsoft Powerpoint Hyperstudio Kid Pix Studio Claris Works Word 　Processing Microsoft Publisher HTML Storybook Weaver	Poster Handwritten report Diorama

Evaluating

	Learning log Reflective journal	Microsoft Word Claris Works Word 　Processing	Handwritten

Name: _____   Date: _____

Understanding my task — checklist

Check the boxes and fill in as many spaces as you can for your task.

* Do I work alone ☐ or in a group? ☐

* Starting date? _____

* Who is my audience? _____

* Do I have any teacher checkpoints? _____

* What do I have to hand in with the final copy?

Task sheet ☐   Research notes ☐   Working disk ☐   Bibliography ☐

* What will my final presentation be? **oral** ☐   **written** ☐   **visual** ☐

oral

    * How long will my talk be? _____ minutes.

    * What other posters/interesting items/people will I use in my talk?

    _____

written

    * What format will I use?   handwritten ☐   word processed ☐

    * How long will it be? _____

visual

    * What format will I use?

      poster ☐   photos ☐   model/construction ☐

      video ☐   multimedia ☐   other _____

Defining: Understands the topic

Name: Date:

What I already know about ....

     ➡ _____

          _____

     ➡ _____

          _____

     ➡ _____

          _____

Questions I think I'll need to answer...

Who? What? Where? When? Why? How?

     ➡ _____

          _____

          _____

     ➡ _____

          _____

     ➡ _____

          _____

     ➡ _____

          _____

Defining: Brainstorming

Name: _____   Date: _____

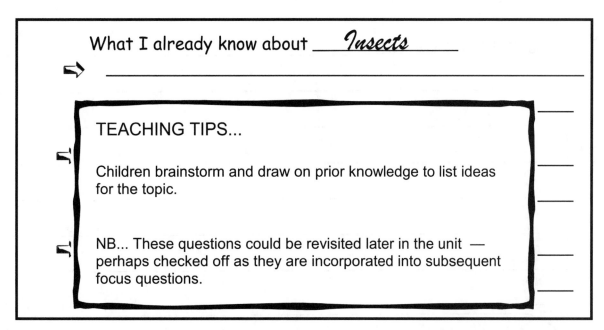

What I already know about _____ *Insects* _____

⇒ _____

> ### TEACHING TIPS...
>
> Children brainstorm and draw on prior knowledge to list ideas for the topic.
>
> NB... These questions could be revisited later in the unit — perhaps checked off as they are incorporated into subsequent focus questions.

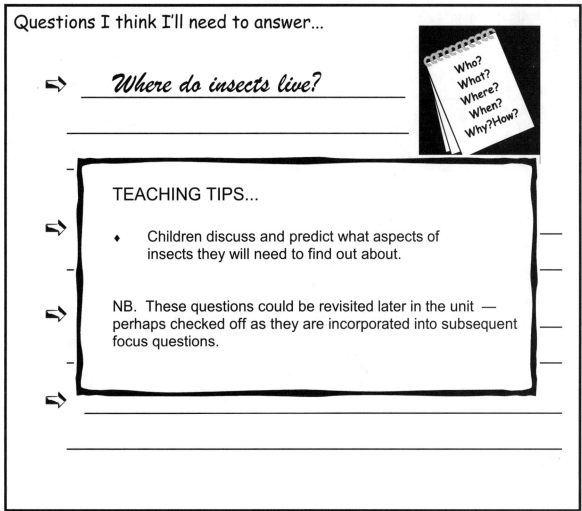

Questions I think I'll need to answer...

⇒ _*Where do insects live?*_ _____

Who? What? Where? When? Why? How?

> ### TEACHING TIPS...
>
> ♦ Children discuss and predict what aspects of insects they will need to find out about.
>
> NB. These questions could be revisited later in the unit — perhaps checked off as they are incorporated into subsequent focus questions.

⇒ _____

_____

Defining: Brainstorming

Name: _____   Date: _____

What I already know about _____

_____

_____

_____

_____

_____

_____

Brainstorming:

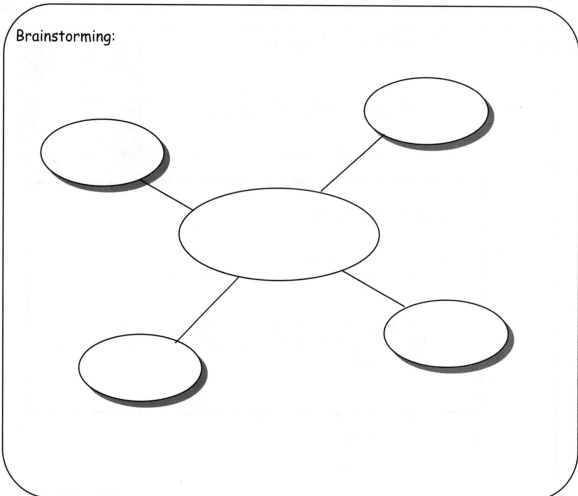

Defining: Draws on prior knowledge/brainstorms — Concept map

Name: _____ Date: _____

What I already know about _____

TEACHING TIPS...

Constructing the subheadings...

Example of LEARNING ACTIVITY...

- From previous Hot Potato, or other Brainstorming activity, Teacher leads children to suggest what aspects (Subheadings) "We need to find out about", e.g., in Fairytale unit — characters, settings, elements of magic, story/plot.

- This activity could be done as a joint construction with the blackline master being used as an

  OVERHEAD TRANSPARENCY

- Children would complete their own worksheet from the Overhead Transparency

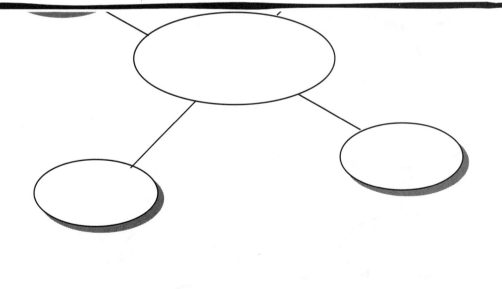

Defining: Draws on prior knowledge/brainstorms — Concept map

Name: Date:

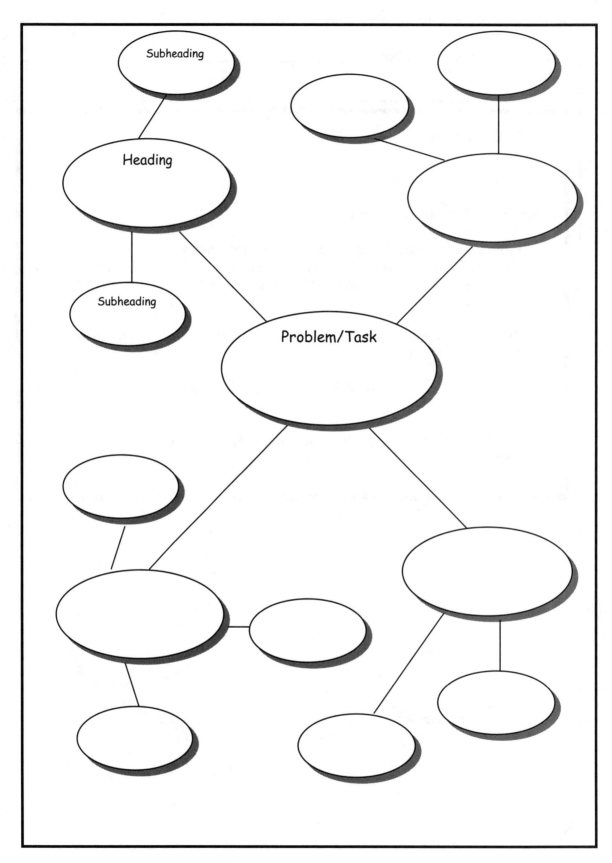

Defining: Brainstorming — Concept map

Name: Date:

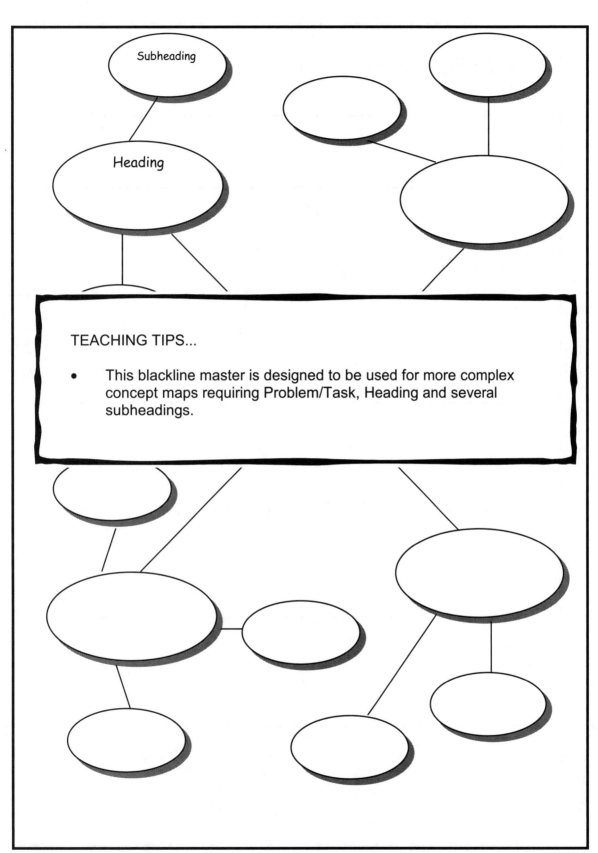

Defining: Brainstorming — Concept map

Name: Date:

| What we know about... |
| _____ |

*

*

*

*

*

*

Defining: Draws on prior knowledge to brainstorm key ideas

Name: _____   Date: _____

What we know about...

_____

TEACHING TIPS...

Hot Potato
- In groups of up to 6 children per group, each child adds 1 piece of information to sheet of paper.

- Information (Key words) is listed in **note form.**

- A class summary of all information on group sheets is made by Teacher.

Example of LEARNING ACTIVITY...

- Children list all elements of Fairy Tales they know, e.g., contain magic, begin with "Once upon a time ... "

*

*

Defining: Draws on prior knowledge to brainstorm key ideas

Name: Date:

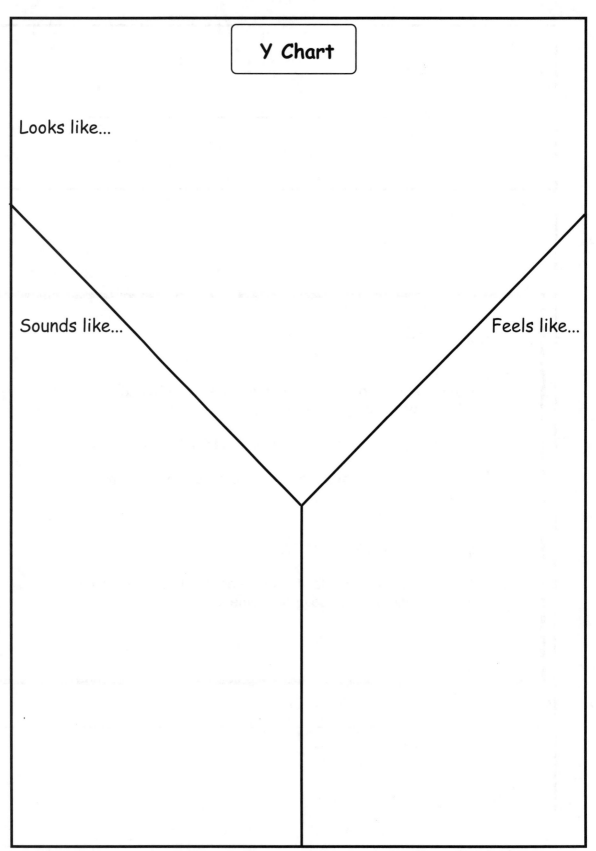

Y Chart

Looks like...

Sounds like...

Feels like...

Defining: Draws on prior knowledge/brainstorms

Name: _____   Date: _____

Y Chart

Looks like...

TEACHING TIPS...

- The Y chart is a method of brainstorming that addresses the affective domain, and is useful for discussion and analysis requiring emotive responses.
  Example: What sort of "climate" students want for their room.

- Relies on the senses — right brain stimulus.

- To be used only as a group activity.

- Use as an Overhead Transparency.

Looks like...
Brainstorm all the good things you would expect to see happening in a particular situation — looking at factors contributing to the value of a situation.

Sounds like...
Brainstorm all the sounds associated with an effective situation or person, e.g., good communication, encouragement, praise, etc.

Feels like...
Include aspects of emotions and kinesthetic responses, e.g., fear, happiness, and feelings of commitment, pride, success, etc.

Defining: Draws on prior knowledge/brainstorms

Name: _____   Date: _____

Questions I think I'll need to answer...

* _____
  _____
  _____

* _____
  _____
  _____
  _____

* _____
  _____
  _____

* _____
  _____
  _____

Who? What?
When?
Where?
How?
Why?

Where will I find the information I need?

People _____ Places _____ Objects _____

School library ☐   Local library ☐   Home ☐

Book ☐   Encyclopedia ☐   Magazine ☐

Video ☐   CD-ROM ☐   Internet ☐

Other _____

Defining: Makes predictions about likely sources of information

Name: _____ **Date:** _____

Questions I think I'll need to answer...

* _____
  _____
  _____

* _____

Who? What?
When?
Where?
How?
Why?

TEACHING TIPS...

- Students brainstorm task using the "6 W's" Framework:

  Who? What? When? Where? How? Why?

- Discuss locating resources with class group to explore possibilities for this particular problem. Some tasks would require specific resources, e.g., for current issues, the internet and magazines would provide more up-to-date information than books.

Where will I find the information I need?

People _____ Places _____ Objects _____

School library ☐   Local library ☐   Home ☐

Book ☐   Encyclopedia ☐   Magazine ☐

Video ☐   CD-ROM ☐   Internet ☐

Other _____

Defining: Makes predictions about likely sources of information

Name: Date:

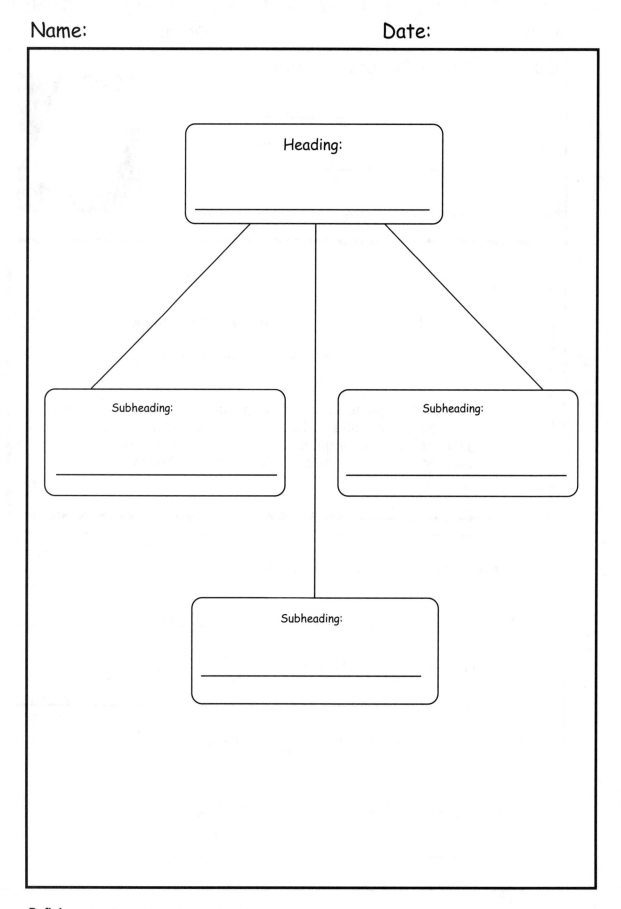

Defining: Identifies main ideas (subheadings)

Name: _____   Date: _____

```
┌─────────────────────────────┐
│        Heading:             │
│                             │
│  _____  │
└─────────────────────────────┘
```

TEACHING TIPS...

Constructing Subheadings (Aspects) of the task.

Example of LEARNING ACTIVITY

This blackline master has been designed to be used as an

OVERHEAD TRANSPARENCY

♦ This activity follows the Brainstorming/Predicting activity.

Through Teacher-led whole group discussion, children devise appropriate Subheadings for the Heading, e.g., using the predictions children have made, lead the children to devise suitable subheadings which describe their questions. Each subheading is a part of the task "that we need to find out about."

Defining: Identifies main ideas (subheadings)

Name: _____ Date: _____

Heading: _____

Subheading: _____ Focus question: _____
Subheading: _____ Focus question: _____
Subheading: _____ Focus question: _____
Subheading: _____ Focus question: _____

Defining: Organizes focus questions into headings

Name: _____ Date: _____

Heading: _____

Subheading: _____

Focus question:_____

> ## TEACHING TIPS...
>
> Using Subheadings from previous activities, questions relating to the subheadings are now developed, e.g., "What questions do we need to ask that will help us to find out about this part of our topic?"
>
> In order to guide the discussion, Focus Questions are best pre-planned by the Teacher.
>
> Example of LEARNING ACTIVITY...
>
> • At this level, Focus Questions would be developed as a joint construction through Teacher-led discussion.
>
> • This blackline master has been designed for use as an
>
>   OVERHEAD TRANSPARENCY
>
> • The worksheet could be used by children to record the Focus Questions devised by the Teacher and class.

Defining: Organizes focus questions into headings

Name: _____   Date: _____

Bookmark

Cut around the outside of the bookmark.
Design and draw a logo for the bottom sections of your bookmark.
Gently score with scissors, or fold, along center line. Glue together.

**Problem solving/
completing a task**

Define the problem...
What exactly do I have to do?

Locate resources...
Where will I find the information I need?

Select/Analyze...
Which of these resources will be of use to me?

Organize/Synthesize...
How can I best organize my information to solve my problem/complete my task?

Create/Present...
How can I best present my solution?

Evaluate...
How effectively did I complete my task?

Choosing a book that's...
just right for **you**

 Five Finger Test

1] Read the first page or couple of pages

2] As you read, when you come to a word you don't know, or can't work out the meaning from the rest of the sentence, fold down one finger.

3] If you have folded all your fingers and thumb on one hand to make a fist by the time you have finished the first page or so, then perhaps the book is a little hard for you just at this time.

4] Try reading the book later on when you're sure to enjoy it more.
✓✓✓

Name:

Name:

Defining: Analyzes and clarifies a given task/Assesses readability of materials

Name: _____   Date: _____

Bookmark

Cut around the outside of the bookmark.

Design and draw a logo for the bottom sections of your bookmark.

Gently score with scissors, or fold, along center line. Glue together.

👍 **Problem solving/**

Choosing a book that's...

just right for **you**

Name:

TEACHING TIPS...

• Photocopy onto colored card.

• Use during introduction to task when revising steps in the Information Process.

• Use Five Finger Test for reading groups and when revising effective selection of reading materials for class groups.

Organize/Synthesize...
How can I best organize my informa tion to solve my problem/complete my task?

Create/Present...
How can I best present my solution?

Evaluate...
How effectively did I complete my task?

3] If you have folded all your fingers and thumb on one hand to make a fist by the time you have finished the first page or so, then perhaps the book is a little hard for you just at this time.

4] Try reading the book later on when you're sure to enjoy it more.
✓✓✓

Name:

Defining: Analyzes and clarifies a given task/Assesses readability of materials

Name: _____   Date: _____

Shelf or spine label: Author:

[ ]   [ ]

            Title:

            [ ]

Spine:

[ ]

        Front cover illustration:

        [ ]

Defining: Understands/uses terminology — Author, Title, Illustration, Spine, Spine/Shelf label

TEACHING TIPS...

- Children are led to understand that:
  E denotes Easy Fiction — one of several locations in library;

- First letter of the Spine/Shelf label comes from the first letter of the author's last name — the first 3 letters of the author's last name are used on the spine/shelf label;

- E is arranged in alphabetical order of authors;

- Story books (Narratives) "live" in E;

- E books usually contain more pictures than words;

- Numbers are used for Nonfiction in another location in the library;

- Books which give us information are kept in Nonfiction;

- Information books are grouped by subject and are arranged in number order;

- Either term, "Spine label" or "Shelf label," is used for the label to denote "where the book lives in the library" (the address of the book).

Example of LEARNING ACTIVITY... (Book cover)

- Children complete boxes, cut and paste onto separate 8 1/2 x 11 paper to make book cover relating to theme, e.g., for author study unit on Stephane Poulin, children could choose *Could you stop Josephine?* to make the book cover.

Defining: Understands/uses terminology—Author, Title, Illustration, Spine, Spine/Shelf label

Name: _____   **Date:** _____

Title:

Author:

Series:

Defining: Understands/uses terminology — Publisher, Series, Contents, Index

TEACHING TIPS...

Book Cover

Example of LEARNING ACTIVITY...
Children:

- Insert author (self), title, spine information, publisher, series;

- Use another folded 8 1/2 x 11 sheet of paper to complete a Contents Page, and an Index. Both Contents and Index should relate to the same unit;

- Illustrate front cover;

- Draw spine/shelf label on the book in the location used in the school library.   (It is very effective to use actual spine labels, if these can be obtained from the library).

- Children write spine/shelf labels —
  For Nonfiction topics, children decide on the appropriate Dewey Number by looking at other books on the same subject in the library.

Series:

Defining: Understands/uses terminology — Publisher, Series, Contents, Index

Name: _____   Date: _____

Easy Fiction books	Nonfiction books

Locating: Differentiates between Easy Fiction and Nonfiction

Name: _____   **Date:** _____

Easy Fiction Books	Nonfiction Books

TEACHING TIPS ...

Preselect both Easy Fiction and Nonfiction resources relating to the teaching topic.

Example of LEARNING ACTIVITY...

- Discuss differences between Fiction (narrative/made up) stories and books containing information (Information/Nonfiction books) — exceptions being Folklore, Poetry, and Literature.

- Demonstrate simple scanning techniques —
  "What can I find out about this book by looking at ..."
  cover, title, illustrations.   (See Selecting/Analyzing)

- Mix together preselected Easy Fiction and Nonfiction books.

- Children select a book, identify as either Easy Fiction or Nonfiction using modeled scanning techniques.

- Children draw front cover of the selected book in a box in the appropriate column.

- Discuss reasons for decision.

- Repeat with remaining boxes.

Locating: Differentiates between Easy Fiction and Nonfiction

Name: **Date:**

Browser card

Illustrate your browser card then cut it out.

Name:

Locating: Locates resources — use of Browser Card

Name: _____   Date: _____

TEACHING TIPS ...

This activity is extremely effective if the Browser Cards can be laminated and kept in the Library for use by all students. They are intended to be used as "place-holders" when students remove books from shelves.

Use in conjunction with teaching unit, e.g., Environments unit — farm environment

Example of LEARNING ACTIVITY...

- children choose a book relating to a farm environment, e.g., *Could you stop Josephine?* by Stephane Poulin.

- illustrate browser card with characters or scenes from *Could you stop Josephine?*

- may also be used when introducing children to the Nonfiction section of the library where book location is more specific than perhaps in Easy Fiction.

Browser card

Illustrate your browser

Name: _____

Locating: Locates resources — use of Browser Card

Name: _____ Date: _____

Spine or shelf label	Subject (What the book's about)

Locating: Uses spine/shelf label to identify resources

Spine or shelf label	Subject

TEACHING TIPS ...

Using Nonfiction books relating to unit theme, children identify relationship between Dewey (Shelf Numbers) and Subject (content of book).

Example of LEARNING ACTIVITY...

- From preselected theme-based resources, children:

 - choose a book, copy details of shelf label on book into "Spine or Shelf label" box on sheet;

 - scan book and write brief description of subject of book ("What the book's about")

Locating: Uses spine/shelf label to identify resources

Locating resources ...

Focus question:_____
_____

Search terms:_____

Resources that might be useful...

1] Author:_____

   Title: _____

   Location

   Available for loan?   Yes/No

   Located on shelf?   Yes/No   _____

                                            _____

2] Author:_____

   Title: _____

   Location

   Available for loan?   Yes/No

   Located on shelf?   Yes/No   _____

                                            _____

3] Author:_____

   Title: _____

   Location

   Available for loan?   Yes/No

   Located on shelf?   Yes/No   _____

                                            _____

Locating: Uses shelf label from author, title, subject, series search to locate resources

Locating resources ...

TEACHING TIPS ...

Use when searching catalog for resources relating to task.

- Brainstorm and write down search term (subject, author, title, etc).

- Type in search term and locate catalog entry for likely resources.

- Note author, title, availability, etc.

- Write down Shelf location/Call No.   e.g.,   NF 599.4 DUG   or   599.4 DUG

- Look on shelves for resources - Note on Worksheet if found.

- Use information from this sheet for Bibliography.

Title: _____

                               Location

Available for loan?   Yes/No

Located on shelf?   Yes/No   _____
                                           _____
                                           _____

2] Author: _____

Title: _____

                               Location

Available for loan?   Yes/No

Located on shelf?   Yes/No   _____
                                           _____
                                           _____

Locating: Uses shelf label from author, title, subject, series search to locate resources

Name: _____   Date: _____

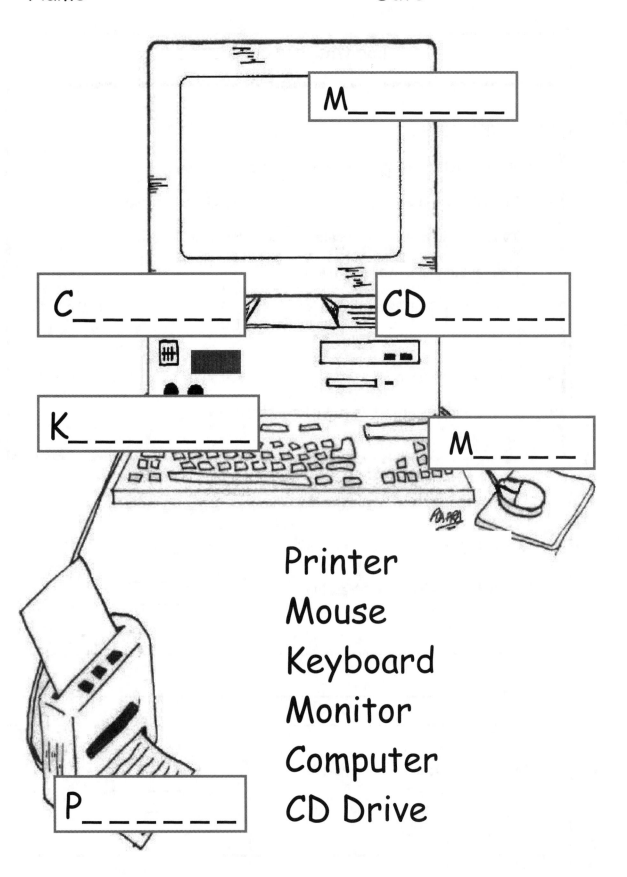

M_____

C_____   CD_____

K_____

M_____

Printer
Mouse
Keyboard
Monitor
Computer
CD Drive

P_____

Locating: Understands and uses computer terminology

Name: _____ Date: _____

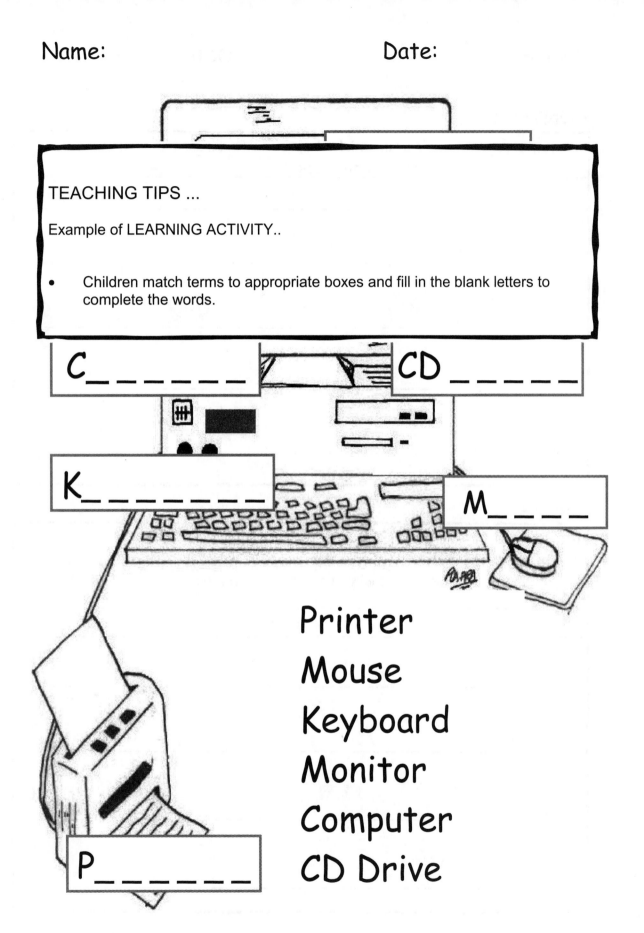

TEACHING TIPS ...

Example of LEARNING ACTIVITY..

• Children match terms to appropriate boxes and fill in the blank letters to complete the words.

C_ _ _ _ _ _ _

CD _ _ _ _ _ _

K_ _ _ _ _ _ _ _

M_ _ _ _ _

Printer

Mouse

Keyboard

Monitor

Computer

CD Drive

P_ _ _ _ _ _ _

Locating: Understands and uses computer terminology

Name: _____   Date: _____

CONTENTS...

Contents page:	Tells us in **which chapter** to find information, usually at the front of the book.	
	Contents	**Page**
Chapter 1	_____	_____
Chapter 2	_____	_____
Chapter 3	_____	_____
Chapter 4	_____	_____

INDEX...

Index page:	Tells us exactly on **which page** (in alphabetical order) to find information, usually at the back of the book .	
	Index	**Page**
a	_____	_____
f	_____	_____
h	_____	_____
m	_____	_____

Locating: Uses Contents/Index page

Name: _____   Date: _____

CONTENTS...

TEACHING TIPS ...

Example of LEARNING ACTIVITY...

- Using preselected book relating to unit theme,
  e.g., Insects, children complete contents section of sheet.

- Using the same book relating to the theme, children locate an entry in the
  Index beginning with the letter on the Worksheet. Discussion can then take
  place comparing the specific entry found in the Index to the more general
  entry of the contents.

INDEX...

Index page: Tells us exactly on **which page** (in alphabetical order) to find
information, usually at the back of the book .

	Index	Page
a	_____	_____
f	_____	_____
h	_____	_____
m	_____	_____

Locating: Uses Contents/Index page

Name: **Date:**

✉ Send	

To: [   ]

Subject: [   ]

[   ]

Locating: Is aware of e-mail communication

Name: Date:

✉ Send

TEACHING TIPS ...

Use as whole class activity to draft message when introducing e-mail for the first time, or subsequently to draft e-mails prior to actually typing message into the computer.

Send - Click on this icon when letter is completed and ready to send to another computer.

To - Address of the person to whom you are sending the e-mail. Addresses for e-mail always contain @.

Subject - A few words to describe contents of letter.

Example of LEARNING ACTIVITY...

- Correspond with e-pals — discuss fairytales, etc.

- Correspond as a class with Teachers, members of class at home addresses.

Locating: Is aware of e-mail communication

Name: _____   Date: _____

Interview grid			
Questions	A	B	C
Names	Answers	Answers	Answers

Locating: Gathers data from simple interviews

Name: _____   **Date:** _____

Interview grid			

TEACHING TIPS ...

- Examples of appropriate questions should be modeled before questions to be asked by students are entered on sheet.

- Names on interviewees should also be entered on sheet prior to interview.

Locating: Gathers data from simple interviews

Name: _____   Date: _____

Researching from a CD-ROM

Heading: _____

Focus question: _____

Search terms: _____

Open program → Search term → Search → Take notes

Notes

Key word: _____

Sentence: _____

_____

Key word: _____

Sentence: _____

_____

Key word: _____

Sentence: _____

_____

Key word: _____

Sentence: _____

_____

Locating: Uses special reference tools — Reference CD-ROM

Name: _____   Date: _____

Researching from a CD-ROM

Heading: _____

TEACHING TIPS ...

This blackline master is designed for use when introducing notetaking from a CD-ROM encyclopedia. Notetaking from a screen is more difficult than notetaking from text and requires some practice.

- Brainstorm search terms.

- Detailed discussion needs to take place regarding text movement, hyperlinks, diagram/picture enlargements and other features specific to particular programs.

Key word: _____

Sentence: _____

_____

Key word: _____

Sentence: _____

_____

Key word: _____

Sentence: _____

_____

Key word: _____

Sentence: _____

_____

Locating: Uses special reference tools — Reference CD-ROM

Name: Date:

Researching from an Encyclopedia

Heading: _____

Focus question: _____

_____

Search terms: _____

| Index | → | Note Vol., Page/s | → | Locate article subheading | → | Take notes |

Notes

Key word: _____

Sentence: _____

_____

Key word: _____

Sentence: _____

_____

Key word: _____

Sentence: _____

_____

Key word: _____

Sentence: _____

_____

Locating: Uses special reference tools — Encyclopedia

Name: _____   Date: _____

Researching from an Encyclopedia

Heading: _____

```
TEACHING TIPS...

This blackline master is designed for use when introducing notetaking from an
encyclopedia.

•    Brainstorm search terms.

•    Use buttons as guide to steps in locating relevant article.
```

Key word: _____

Sentence: _____

_____

Key word: _____

Sentence: _____

_____

Key word: _____

Sentence: _____

_____

Key word: _____

Sentence: _____

_____

Locating: Uses special reference tools — Encyclopedia

Name: _____   Date: _____

Researching from a Bookmarked Internet site

Heading: _____

Focus question: _____
_____

Search terms: _____

| Internet icon | → | Bookmarks/ Favorites | → | Internet site | → | Take notes |

👆   Hyperlink — Click to move to another page

⇐   Back — Click to go back one screen

Side bar — Use arrows to scroll down screen

Notes

Key word: _____

Sentence: _____
_____

Key word: _____

Sentence: _____
_____

Key word: _____

Sentence: _____
_____

Locating: Uses special reference tools — Internet sites

Name: _____ Date: _____

Researching from a Bookmarked Internet site

Heading: _____

Focus question: _____

_____

Search terms: _____

Internet icon → Bookmarks/ Favorites → Internet site → Take notes

👆 Hyperlink — Click to move to another page

⇐ Back — Click to go back one screen

Side bar — Use arrows to scroll down screen

Notes

Key word: _____

TEACHING TIPS ...

This blackline master is designed for use when introducing Bookmarked Internet sites.

- Brainstorm search terms.

- Use buttons as guide to steps in locating relevant articles.

- Model use of appropriate browser icons,
  e.g., Internet Explorer icon or Netscape Navigator icon.

Locating: Uses special reference tools — Internet sites

Name: _____   Date: _____

Researching from an Atlas

Heading: _____

Focus question: _____

_____

Search terms: _____

| Index | → | Search term | → | Map reference | → | Record coordinates |

Search term (location)	Map Page	Coordinates

Locating: Uses special reference tools — Atlas

Name: _____   Date: _____

Researching from an Atlas

Heading: _____

Focus question: _____

_____

Search terms: _____

| Index | → | Search term | → | Map reference | → | Record coordinates |

Search term (location)	Map Page	Coordinates

TEACHING TIPS ...

This blackline master is designed to be used for modeling purposes (perhaps as an overhead transparency) when introducing the use of the Atlas as a source of information, then subsequently by students for practice and revision of the learned skills.

Locating: Uses special reference tools — Atlas

Name: _____ Date: _____

Using a Telephone Directory

Heading: _____

Focus question: _____

_____

Search terms: _____

Use alphabetical order of surnames → Locate Guide words at top of page → Locate surname

Surname	Address	Phone number

Locating: Uses special reference tools — Telephone directory

Name: _____   Date: _____

Using a Telephone Directory

Heading: _____

Focus question: _____

_____

Search terms: _____

Use alphabetical order of surnames	→	Locate Guide words at top of page	→	Locate surname

Surname	Address	Phone number

TEACHING TIPS ...

Use this blackline master within the context of the set problem or task to locate names, addresses or phone numbers as relevant.

- Search term would be the name of person or organization.

- When using Yellow Pages, Index should be searched first using search terms.

Locating: Uses special reference tools — Telephone directory

Name: _____ Date: _____

NONFICTION BOOK REVIEW

Author: _____

Title: _____

Location: _____
_____

Organization

	Yes/No
* Index	☐
* Contents	☐
* Glossary	☐

Text (Words)

	Yes/No
* Easy to read	☐
* Right size	☐
* Useful information	☐

Photos/illustrations/diagrams

	Yes/No		Yes/No
* Interesting	☐	* Near relevant text	☐
* Useful	☐	* Captions/labels	☐

I thought this book was_____

_____

_____

Selecting/Analyzing: Evaluates appropriateness of resources

Name: _____ Date: _____

NONFICTION BOOK REVIEW

Author: _____

Title: _____

Location: _____
_____
_____

Organization

	Yes/No
* Index	
* Contents	
* Glossary	

Text (Words)

	Yes/No
* Easy to read	
* Right size	
* Useful information	

Photos/illustrations/diagrams

	Yes/No		Yes/No
* Interesting		* Near relevant text	

TEACHING TIPS ...

Students learn to be discerning in the choice of text resources.

How accessible is the information?

Does the book contain the appropriate tools to access the information?

Selecting/Analyzing: Evaluates appropriateness of resources

Name: _____ Date: _____

This is a picture of

_____

who knows a lot about

_____

This is what I found out...

Name: _____ **Date:** _____

This is a picture of

_____

who knows a lot about

_____

This is what I found out...

TEACHING TIPS ...
- Use when a visitor (Primary source) talks to class, e.g., Career unit —
  Shopkeeper, Doctor, etc.

- Children may either draw or write their information.

Selecting/Analyzing: Is aware of people with special knowledge as a Primary resource

Name: Date:

This is a picture of

_____

who knows a lot about

_____

I found out that...   _____

Selecting/Analyzing: Is aware of people with special knowledge as a Primary resource

Name: **Date:**

This is a picture of

_____

who knows a lot about

_____

I found out that... _____

_____

_____

_____

TEACHING TIPS ...

- Use when a visitor to the school (Primary source) talks to class, e.g. Bee-keeper parent.

- Use for excursions when an "expert" talks to class, e.g., Museum Guide.

Selecting/Analyzing: Is aware of people with special knowledge as a Primary resource

Name: Date:

This is what interested me most when we visited...

_____

This is what I found out...

Selecting/Analyzing: Is aware of special places, objects as a Primary resource

Name: _____   Date: _____

This is what interested me most when we visited...
_____ *our neighborhood* _____

This is what I found out...

TEACHING TIPS ...

- Use for excursions, e.g., Farm, Neighborhood — (Environments unit), etc.

- Children either draw or write.

Selecting/Analyzing: Is aware of special places, objects as a Primary resource

Name: Date:

These are some of the interesting things I observed when ...

_____

This is what I found out...

Selecting/Analyzing: Is aware of special places, objects as a Primary resource

Name: Date:

These are some of the interesting things I observed when ...

we had an insect display in our room.

This is what I found out..

Insects have 6 legs.

TEACHING TIPS ...

- Use when a class display is set up — e.g., specimens collected by children or loan from Museum.

- Useful follow-up to an excursion, e.g., to Museum.

Selecting/Analyzing: Is aware of special places, objects as a Primary resource

Name: _____ **Date:** _____

First... ————————————————————
————————————————————————————————

┌──────────────────────────────────────┐
│   │
│   │
│   │
│   │
│   │
└──────────────────────────────────────┘

Then... ————————————————————
————————————————————————————————

┌──────────────────────────────────────┐
│   │
│   │
│   │
│   │
│   │
└──────────────────────────────────────┘

Afterwards... ————————————————
————————————————————————————————

┌──────────────────────────────────────┐
│   │
│   │
│   │
│   │
│   │
└──────────────────────────────────────┘

Selecting/Analyzing: Arranges ideas, events, facts in sequence

Name: _____ **Date:** _____

First... _____

_____

```
┌─────────────────────────────────────────┐
│                                           │
│                                           │
│                                           │
│                                           │
│                                           │
└─────────────────────────────────────────┘
```

Then... _____

_____

TEACHING TIPS ...
Link to Recount structure.

Children dictate to Teacher, or children write explanation of pictures.

Example of LEARNING ACTIVITY...

- Using information gained during teaching of Unit, children complete Story Map to sequence ideas, events, facts, e.g.,

    - recounts of excursions could be written or recorded using illustrations;

    - life cycles recorded;

    - milking cow, baling hay, etc., recorded.

Selecting/Analyzing: Arranges ideas, events, facts in sequence

Name: _____   Date: _____

First... _____

_____

_____

_____

_____

Then... _____

_____

_____

_____

_____

Afterwards... _____

_____

_____

_____

_____

Selecting/Analyzing: Arranges ideas, events, facts in sequence

Name: _____   Date: _____

First... _____

_____

_____

_____

_____

Then... _____

_____

_____

TEACHING TIPS ...

Link to Recount OR Narrative structure.

Example of LEARNING ACTIVITY...

Using information gained during teaching of the Unit, children complete Story Map to sequence ideas, events, facts, e.g., in a problem or task relating to Insects ...

• narrative — e.g., use *The very hungry caterpillar* by Eric Carle; for modeled example;

• recounts of excursions, e.g,, to museum;

• life cycles — e.g., Big Book: *Eggs and life cycles* (Scholastic) for modeled example.

Selecting/Analyzing: Arranges ideas, events, facts in sequence

Name: _____   Date: _____

Timeline for... _____

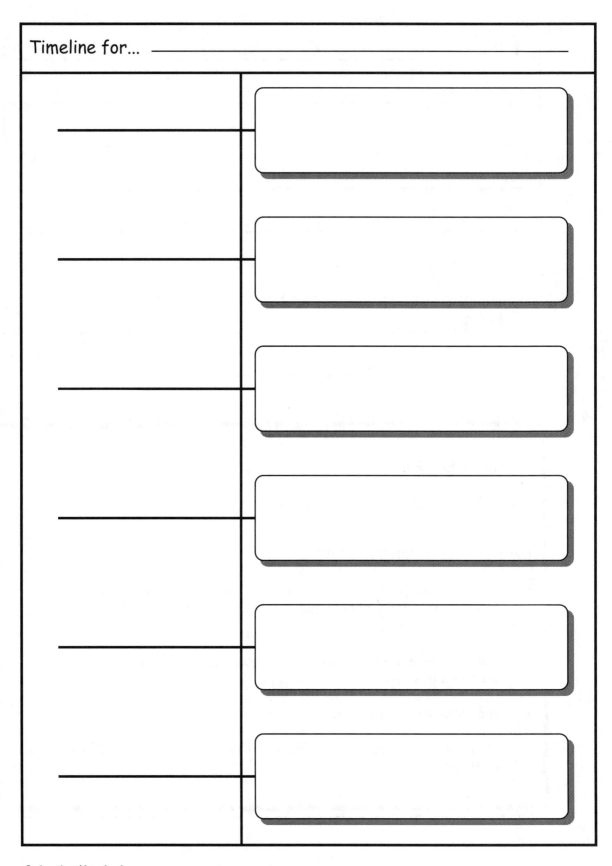

Selecting/Analyzing: Arranges ideas, facts, events in sequence

Name: _____   Date: _____

Timeline for... _____

____	[ ]
____	[ ]
____	[ ]
	[ ]

TEACHING TIPS ...

Example of LEARNING ACTIVITY...

- may be used for recording of information, e.g., growth of plant;

- time sequencing of narrative,e.g., Story map (Fairytale unit) — *Hansel and Gretel*

Selecting/Analyzing: Arranges ideas, facts, events in sequence

Name: Date:

Bibliography

Book:

Author	Date	Title	Publisher

Encyclopedia:

Title	Date	Volume No.

CD-ROM:

Title	Date	Publisher

Internet:

Author	Title of Entry	http	Date of download

Selecting/Analyzing: Records bibliographic sources of information

Name: _____   Date: _____

Bibliography

Book:

Author	Date	Title	Publisher

Encyclopedia:

Title	Date	Volume No.

CD-ROM:

> TEACHING TIPS ...
>
> Students record the bibliographic information **as they use** each resource.
>
> During the selection process in the Selecting/Analyzing stage, students should have entered details of all relevant resources on this worksheet. Additional records would be added during the Organizing/Synthesizing stage if needed.

Selecting/Analyzing: Records bibliographic sources of information

Name: _____   Date: _____

Subheading:	_____
Focus question:	_____

Key words

_____

_____

_____

My information came from... Title: _____

Subheading:	_____
Focus question:	_____

Key words

_____

_____

_____

My information came from... Title: _____

Selecting/Analyzing: Identifies key words

Name: Date:

Subheading: *Homes*

Focus question: *Where do insects live?*

Key words

under bark of trees

TEACHING TIPS ...

Discuss Focus questions, Subheadings, Key words...

- **Focus questions** are the questions we need to answer to find out about this part of our task, e.g.,

  > Where do insects live?;
  > What do insects eat?;
  > What is special about insects?

- We use Focus questions because it's easier to find answers to questions than to a subheading, e.g., "Where do insects live?" / "Homes."

  (It is useful to have one general focus question that can incorporate Key words the children have identified that do not fit into any other of the specific focus questions.)

- **Subheadings** (usually a word or short phrase) are what the focus questions are about, e.g., Homes, Food, Special characteristics.

- **Key words** are the important words which are **short answers** to our focus questions.

Selecting/Analyzing: Identifies key words

Name: _____   **Date:** _____

Subheading: _____

Focus question: _____

Key words

_____

_____

_____

_____

My information came from... Title: _____

by... (Author): _____

Subheading: _____

Focus question: _____

Key words

_____

_____

_____

_____

My information came from... Title: _____

by... (Author): _____

Selecting/Analyzing: Lists key words under subheadings (main ideas)

Name: _____   Date: _____

Subheading: _____

Focus question: _____

| Key words | _____ |

_____

_____

_____

My information came from... Title: _____

by... (Author): _____

Subheading: _____

Focus question: _____

TEACHING TIPS ...

This worksheet has been included for those students whose responses are more detailed.

- It is very important that the students always record subheadings and focus questions where relevant.

- Students would require 2 copies of this page where they are dealing with 4 subheadings.

Selecting/Analyzing: Lists key words under subheadings (main ideas)

Name: **Date:**

Subheading: ————————————————————

Focus question: ——————————————————

Key word: ——————————————————

Sentence: ——————————————————

Key word: ——————————————————

Sentence: ——————————————————

Key word: ——————————————————

Sentence: ——————————————————

Key word: ——————————————————

Sentence: ——————————————————

Organizing/Synthesizing: Constructs sentences orally using identified key words.

Name: _____ Date: _____

Subheading: _____ *Homes* _____

Focus question: _____ *Where do insects live?* _____

Key word: _____ *nests* _____

Sentence: _____ *Some insects live in nests.* _____

Key word: _____

Sentence: _____

Key word: _____

TEACHING TIPS ...
At this level, children **would not be constructing sentences independently** from key words.

- This blackline master has been designed for use as an

   OVERHEAD TRANSPARENCY

   for joint construction by the class, and is therefore an **oral activity,** not written.

Organizing/Synthesizing: Constructs sentences orally using identified key words.

Name: _____ Date: _____

Subheading: _____

Focus question: _____

_____

Key word: _____

Sentence: _____

_____

Key word: _____

Sentence: _____

_____

Key word: _____

Sentence: _____

_____

Key word: _____

Sentence: _____

_____

Organizing\Synthesizing: Categorizes information — constructs sentences from key words

Name: _____ Date: _____

Subheading: _____

Focus question: _____

_____

Key word: _____

Sentence: _____

_____

Key word: _____

Sentence: _____

TEACHING TIPS ...

Constructing sentences from key words.

Example of LEARNING ACTIVITY...

- At this level, **extensive modeling and joint construction** of sentences would be appropriate.

- **All resource materials are removed**, so that children understand that the sentences must be constructed to incorporate their key word in answer to the focus question.

- One sentence should be constructed for each key word.

Organizing\Synthesizing: Categorizes information — constructs sentences from key words

Name: Date:

Organizing/Synthesizing: Categorizes information into list format

Name: Date:

Pets	Farm animals

TEACHING TIPS ...

This activity could be done using:

- concrete objects — shapes, animal sets, etc.,

- pictures cut from old magazines;

- children's drawings or writing.

Example of LEARNING ACTIVITY...

- Using example of author unit on Stephane Poulin, children could categorize animals under the headings of "Pets" and "Farm animals."

Organizing/Synthesizing: Categorizes information into list format

Name: _____   **Date:** _____

Organizing/Synthesizing: Categorizes information into list format

Name:	Date:

Insects with wings	*Insects with no wings*

TEACHING TIPS...

Use for information retrieval — compare and contrast.

Example of LEARNING ACTIVITY...

List (write or draw) insects belonging to 2 groups, e.g.,

    Insects that have wings ;
    Insects that have no wings.

Organizing/Synthesizing: Categorizes information into list format

Name: **Date:**

Organizing/Synthesizing: Categorizes information into list format

Name: Date:

Insect	Home	Food

TEACHING TIPS...

Use for comparing and contrasting.

Example of LEARNING ACTIVITY...

- Comparing food and homes of different insects.

Organizing/Synthesizing: Categorizes information into list format

Organizing/Synthesizing: Categorizes information into list format

Name: Date:

Characters	Settings	Elements of magic	Story/Plot
ogres	castles	spells	happy ending

TEACHING TIPS ...

May be used as grid/retrieval chart, e.g., Fairytale unit.

Example of LEARNING ACTIVITY...

- From a selection of books relating to the topic, e.g., Fairytales, list different characters, settings, etc., found in fairytale texts.

Organizing/Synthesizing: Categorizes information into list format

Name: Date:

Heading: _____

Subheading: _____

Paragraph: _____

_____

_____

_____

_____

_____

_____

_____

_____

_____

_____

_____

Organizing/Synthesizing: Synthesizes selected information

Name: _____   Date: _____

Heading: _____

Subheading: _____

Paragraph: _____

_____

_____

_____

_____

_____

TEACHING TIPS...

Each child would require 2 pages (back to back) to write the paragraphs for 4 Subheadings.

At this level, this presentation constitutes the **final copy**.

Example of LEARNING ACTIVITY...

- Children transfer previously completed sentences to develop paragraphs for each subheading.

Organizing/Synthesizing: Synthesizes selected information

Name: _____   Date: _____

_____

_____

Subheading: _____

Paragraph No. [   ] _____

_____

_____

_____

_____

_____

_____

_____

Subheading: _____

Paragraph No. [   ] _____

_____

_____

_____

_____

_____

_____

_____

_____

_____

Organizing/Synthesizing: Categorizes information into a framework of headings

Name: _____   Date: _____

_____

_____

Subheading: _____

Paragraph No. [   ]   _____

_____

_____

_____

_____

_____

_____

_____

TEACHING TIPS ...

- After completing sentences from Key word/Sentence sheet, students construct cohesive paragraphs using the sentences developed from their key words.

- Each sentence should provide the answer to the relevant Focus Question.

_____

_____

_____

_____

_____

Organizing/Synthesizing: Categorizes information into a framework of headings

Name: _____   Date: _____

Time line for: _____

Notes

_____

_____   _____

_____

_____   _____

_____

_____   _____

_____

_____   _____

_____

_____   _____

_____

_____   _____

_____

_____   _____

_____

_____   _____

Organizing/Synthesizing: Organizes ideas and information logically

Name: _____   Date: _____

Time line for: _____*Revolutionary War*_____

April 1775	Notes
Paul Revere's Ride	* *warns colonists the Bristish soldiers were coming*
June 1775	
Battle of Bunker Hill	* *first big battle of the war*
_____	
_____	_____
_____	
_____	_____
_____	

TEACHING TIPS ...

- Students may use this time line to give a time sequence to their research.

- Use it as a visual aid to student learning and improving student understanding of events occurring over a passage of time.

- This blackline master may be used to suit different purposes in a variety of time sequences.

_____	
_____	_____
_____	
_____	_____

Organizing/Synthesizing: Organizes ideas and information logically

Name: _____   Date: _____

Storyboard: _____

1]
2]

3]
4]

5]
6]

Organizing/Synthesizing: Organizes ideas and information logically

Name: _____   Date: _____

Storyboard: _____

1]

2]

3]

4]

Organizing/Synthesizing: Organizes ideas and information logically

Name: Date:

Visitor's name: _____

Occupation: _____

Expert on: _____

I found out...

_____

_____

_____

_____

_____

_____

_____

_____

_____

_____

_____

_____

_____

_____

Organizing/Synthesizing: Makes notes using written bulleted points (List making)

Name: _____   Date: _____

Visitor's name: _____

Occupation: _____

Expert on: _____

I found out...

_____

_____

_____

_____

_____

TEACHING TIPS ...

- Use when a visitor meets with a group of students to talk about his/her field of expertise.

- This blackline master uses list making as a note-taking form. Brief key words are jotted down to be expanded into sentences at a later time.

- Some visitors would prefer that notes be taken following, rather than during, the talk. In this case, it is preferable that the notes be made as soon as possible after the visit.

_____

_____

Organizing/Synthesizing: Makes notes using written bulleted points (List making)

Name: _____   Date: _____

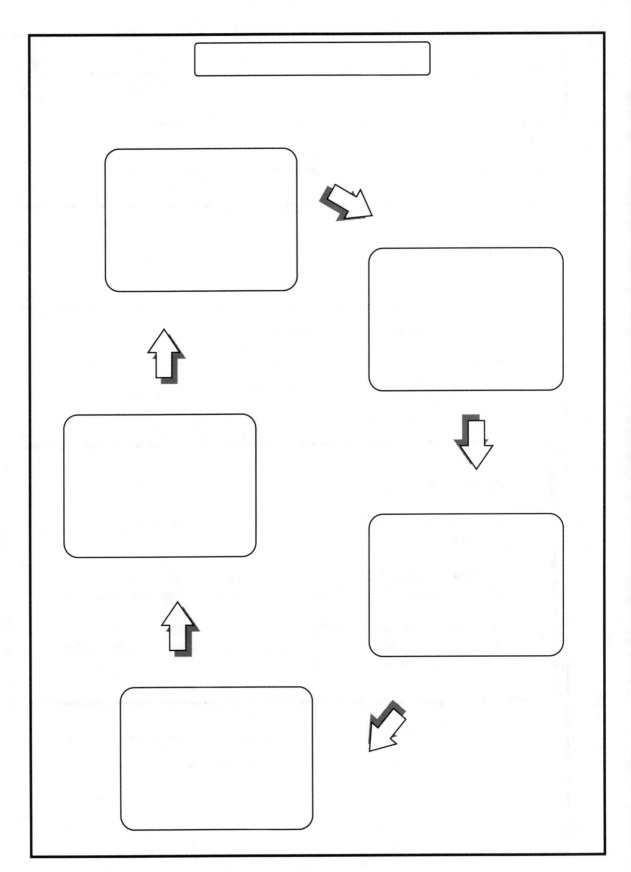

Organizing/Synthesizing: Organizes ideas/information logically — life cycle/food chain

Name: Date:

Life cycle/Food chain

TEACHING TIPS ...

- Arrows are used to indicate direction and structure of text.

- Labels may be used to clarify and supplement illustrations.

- Arrows may also be used to indicate growth, change or time sequence.

- Strength of this diagramatic form lies in a large amount of information being condensed into the cycle framework with a minimum of text.

Organizing/Synthesizing: Organizes ideas/information logically — life cycle/food chain

Name: Date:

Heading: _____

Focus question: _____

Similarities	Differences

Heading: _____

Focus question: _____

Similarities	Differences

Organizing/Synthesizing: Synthesizes selected information connecting similar ideas

Name: _____   Date: _____

Heading: _____

Focus question: _____

Similarities	Differences

TEACHING TIPS ...

- Form of Compare-and-Contrast strategy.

- Useful for analysis of situations — e.g., Our School and a Japanese School;
  analysis of events — Festivals in Australia and Festivals in Europe;
  time comparisons — Holidays in the past and present.

Organizing/Synthesizing: Synthesizes selected information connecting similar ideas

Name: _____   Date: _____

| S.W.O.T. Analysis |

Problem/Task:_____
_____
_____

Strengths:	**W**eaknesses:

Opportunities:	**T**hreats:

Solution A: _____
_____
_____

Solution B: _____
_____
_____

Organizing/Synthesizing: Is aware there may be alternative solutions to a problem

Name: _____   Date: _____

S.W.O.T. Analysis

Problem/Task: _____

_____

_____

Strengths:	**W**eaknesses:

TEACHING TIPS...

S — Strengths of the situation
W — Weaknesses of the situation
O — Opportunities perceived
T — Threats perceived

- Use for analyzing an issue/organization, e.g., Red Cross as an effective organization; or the effectiveness of Student Council.

- Generally, Strengths/Weaknesses may be internal factors, within your control. Opportunities/Threats are external factors, outside your control.

- Strengths: Personal factors — includes motivation, enthusiasm.

- Weaknesses: Requires honest assessment — includes limitations, barriers, defects.

- Opportunities: Look at Weaknesses which may be addressed through outside opportunity, e.g., Joining Drama Group if shyness is a Weakness.

- Threats: Often factors beyond your control. Use Strengths to minimise Threats, e.g., rearranging workload.

_____

_____

_____

Organizing/Synthesizing: Is aware there may be alternative solutions to a problem

Date: _____ Time: _____

Notes/Observations:_____

_____

_____

_____

_____

_____

_____

Date: _____ Time: _____

Notes/Observations:_____

_____

_____

_____

_____

_____

_____

Date: _____ Time: _____

Notes/Observations:_____

_____

_____

_____

_____

_____

_____

Organizing/Synthesizing: Verifies results of experiments

Name: _____   **Date:** _____

_____

Date: ————————   Time: ————————

Notes/Observations:———————————————————————

_____

_____

_____

_____

_____

_____

Date: ————————   Time: ————————

Notes/Observations:———————————————————————

_____

_____

TEACHING TIPS ...

-    Draw object in rectangle; describe change.

- Useful for:
  recording changes — e.g., moon phases, weather;
  growth — e.g., stages of a plant;
  making comparisons — e.g., light/dark;
  observations — e.g., use in conjunction with traffic tally.

_____

_____

_____

_____

_____

_____

Organizing/Synthesizing: Verifies results of experiments

Name: _____   Date: _____

```
┌─────────────────────────────────────────────────────┐
│            ┌───────────────────────────────┐         │
│            │                               │         │
│            └───────────────────────────────┘         │
│   ┌─┐  ┌────────────────────────────────────────┐    │
│   │1│  │                                         │    │
│   └─┘  │                                         │    │
│        │                                         │    │
│        │                                         │    │
│        │                                         │    │
│        └────────────────────────────────────────┘    │
│   ┌─┐  ┌────────────────────────────────────────┐    │
│   │2│  │                                         │    │
│   └─┘  │                                         │    │
│        │                                         │    │
│        │                                         │    │
│        │                                         │    │
│        └────────────────────────────────────────┘    │
│   ┌─┐  ┌────────────────────────────────────────┐    │
│   │3│  │                                         │    │
│   └─┘  │                                         │    │
│        │                                         │    │
│        │                                         │    │
│        └────────────────────────────────────────┘    │
└─────────────────────────────────────────────────────┘
```

Creating/Presenting: Presents information in written and visual sequence

1

2

TEACHING TIPS...
Final presentation to record sequencing of facts, ideas, events in visual or written format.

Example of LEARNING ACTIVITY...

story (narrative) sequencing, e.g., *Very Hungry Caterpillar* by Eric Carle.

• Illustrate using own drawings or pictures cut from magazines.

• Cut and paste "mixed up" 4-part story text into correct sequence.

• Recount sequencing — e.g.,
  video about insects;
  excursion to museum.

• Life cycle of an insect.

Creating/Presenting: Presents information in written and visual sequence

Name: Date:

Creating/Presenting: Presents information in written and visual sequence

Name: _____   **Date:** _____

[_____]

1 | [   ]

2 | [

┌───┐
│ TEACHING TIPS ...   │
│   │
│ •   Children sequence information in either written or visual │
│   format (magazine pictures or drawings)   │
│   │
│ •   Use for the final presentation of written or visual   │
│   response.   │
│   │
│   │
│ Example of LEARNING ACTIVITY..   │
│   │
│ •   Story sequencing, e.g., *Could You Stop Josephine?* by   │
│   Stephane Poulin, could be done using illustrations, or   │
│   cut and paste 4 parts of story text which has been   │
│   "mixed up."   │
│   │
│ •   Recount of excursion, e.g., Neighborhood Walk   │
└───┘

Creating/Presenting: Presents information in written and visual sequence

Name: _____   Date: _____

Planning a Dramatic Presentation

Planning:

Purpose — Why are we presenting this play?_____

_____

Audience — Who will be our audience? _____

_____

Characters	Costumes	Props

Stage Plan

Creating/Presenting: Presents a solution to a problem using a dramatic presentation

Name: _____   Date: _____

Planning a Dramatic Presentation

Planning:

Purpose — Why are we presenting this play?——————————————
_____

Audience — Who will be our audience? ————————————————
_____

Characters	Costumes	Props

TEACHING TIPS...

- This activity represents the culmination of researching a topic and script-writing, or the presentation of a published play.

- This worksheet is designed as a focus for students to plan their presentation.

- Students would need to draw a stage plan for each different setting of the play.

Creating/Presenting: Presents a solution to a problem using a dramatic presentation

Name: _____   Date: _____

Flow chart: _____

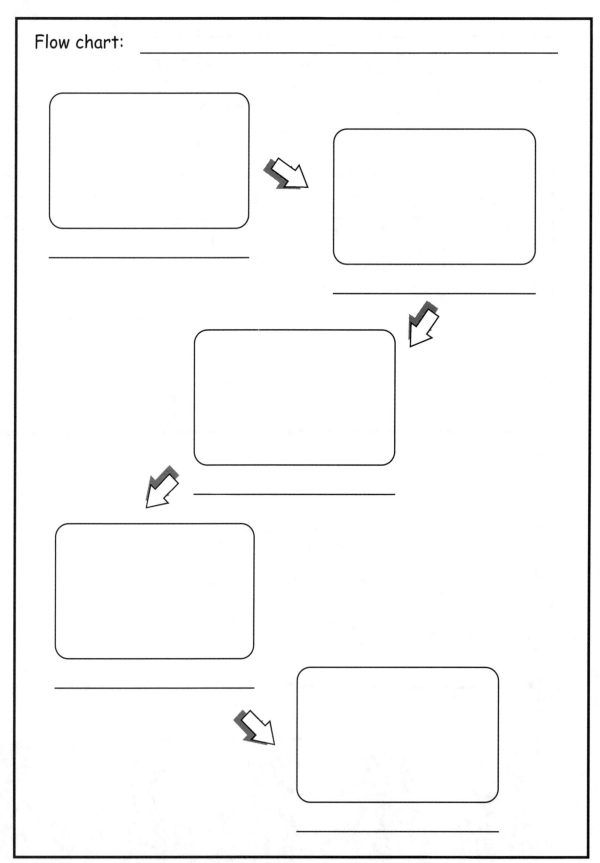

Name: _____   Date: _____

Flow chart: _____

```
┌─────────────────┐            ┌─────────────────┐
│                 │            │                 │
│                 │    ⇘       │                 │
│                 │            │                 │
│                 │            │                 │
└─────────────────┘            │                 │
  _____               └─────────────────┘
                                 _____
                                            ⇘
          ┌─────────────────┐
          │                 │
          │                 │
          │                 │
```

┏━━┓
┃   ┃
┃ TEACHING TIPS...   ┃
┃   ┃
┃ •   Useful for showing connections and relationships, growth or sequencing of ┃
┃   events.   ┃
┃   ┃
┃ •   Summarize a process, e.g., Milking a cow.   ┃
┃   ┃
┃ •   Visual instruction/explanation, e.g., recipe, origami. ┃
┃   ┃
┗━━┛

```
            ⇘
          ┌─────────────────┐
          │                 │
          │                 │
          │                 │
          └─────────────────┘
            _____
```

Creating/Presenting: Creates presentations exhibiting synthesis of information

Name: _____   Date: _____

Flow chart: _____

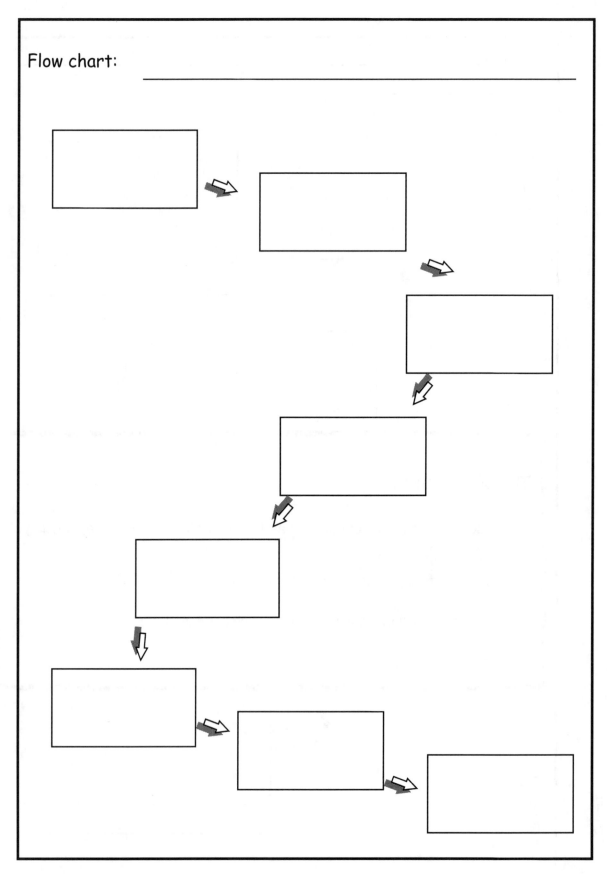

Creating/Presenting: Creates presentations exhibiting synthesis of information

Name: _____ Date: _____

Flow chart: _____

```
┌──────────────┐
│              │
│              │ ⇨  ┌────────────────┐
│              │    │                │
└──────────────┘    │                │
                    │                │ ⇨
                    └────────────────┘   ┌────────────────┐
                                         │                │
                                         │                │
                                         │                │
                                         └────────────────┘ ⇨
                                              ┌─────────┐
```

TEACHING TIPS...

• May be used for text or graphics.

• Information may be written in note form.

• May be completely pictorial sequence.

• Useful for more complex sequences.

• May also be used to depict consequences of an action.

```
┌──────────┐      ┌────────────────┐
│          │ ⇨    │                │
│          │      │                │
└──────────┘      │                │ ⇨   ┌────────────────┐
                  └────────────────┘     │                │
                                         │                │
                                         │                │
                                         └────────────────┘
```

Creating/Presenting: Creates presentations exhibiting synthesis of information

Name: _____   Date: _____

Bar graph: _____

Problem: _____

Each cell represents: _____

Creating/Presenting: Presents a solution to a problem using graphs

Name: _____ Date: _____

Bar graph: _____

Problem: _____

Each cell represents: _____

Creating/Presenting: Presents a solution to a problem using graphs

Name: _____   **Date:** _____

Planning an Oral Presentation

Planning:

Purpose?   Audience?   Planning

Designing:

| Clear, logical information? | Good reasons for my ideas? | Note cards — list of points? |

| More interesting? Posters, models, diagrams | Props? Hat, coat, etc. |

Presenting:

- ✓ DON'T READ note cards.
- ✓ Keep head up and look at audience — make eye contact.
- ✓ Use gestures for emphasis, but don't overdo it.
- ✓ Try to vary voice — volume and pace.
- ✓ Speak loudly enough for those at the back to hear clearly.

Outline for: _____

Introduction: _____

Point 1: _____

Point 2: _____

Point 3: _____

Conclusion: _____

_____

Creating/Presenting: Presents a solution to a problem using simple oral presentation

Name: _____   Date: _____

Planning an Oral Presentation

Planning:

Purpose?   Audience?   Planning

Designing:

| Clear, logical information? | Good reasons for my ideas? | Note cards — list of points? |

| More interesting? Posters, models, diagrams | Props? Hat, coat, etc. |

Presenting:

- ✓ DON'T READ note cards.
- ✓ Keep head up and look at audience — make eye contact.
- ✓ Use gestures for emphasis, but don't overdo it.

TEACHING TIPS...

- Use to guide simple orals.

- Importance of completing the Information Process and planning of an oral should be stressed.

- Notes taken during the research phase are ideal to form the basis of note cards.

- Construction of note cards requires extensive modeling and guidance — entire talk SHOULD NOT be written on note cards.

- Complete sentences SHOULD NOT be used — only notes.

Creating/Presenting: Presents a solution to a problem using simple oral presentation

Name: _____ Date: _____

Planning a Visual Presentation (Poster)

Planning:

Purpose?   Audience?   Layout

Designing:

| Clear, logical information | Text to explain illustrations | Illustrations to support text |

Design tips: (For flexibility, always attach pieces to poster)

To organize:	Heading, Subheading, Column, box, flow chart, label, caption
To emphasize:	Colored lines, colored background, border
To separate:	White space
To connect:	Arrows, lines
To illustrate:	Photo, Cross section, Diagram, Drawing, Graph
	Techniques: Paint, felt pen, pencil, crayon, collage, 3D

Layout plan
for: _____

Notes: _____

_____

_____

_____

_____

_____

_____

_____

_____

_____

_____

Creating/Presenting: Presents a solution to a problem using simple visual presentation

Name: _____   Date: _____

Planning a Visual Presentation (Poster)

Planning:

 Purpose?

 Audience?

Layout

Designing:

| Clear, logical information | Text to explain illustrations | Illustrations to support text |

Design tips: (For flexibility, always attach pieces to poster)

To organize: Heading, Subheading, Column, box, flow chart, label, caption
To emphasize: Colored lines, colored background, border
To separate: White space
To connect: Arrows, lines
To illustrate: Photo, Cross section, Diagram, Drawing, Graph
                         Techniques: Paint, felt pen, pencil, crayon, collage, 3D

Layout
plan for: _____

TEACHING TIPS...

- Use to guide student presentations.

- Emphasis should be placed on planning, e.g., layout should be designed, information should be written/word processed on to separate pieces of paper, then attached to poster following the design plan.

- Importance of using the Information Process prior to completing the poster should be stressed.

Creating/Presenting: Presents a solution to a problem using simple visual presentation

Name: _____   Date: _____

Labeled diagrams are used to:
- ✓ Summarize information using pictures
- ✓ Name parts of a picture clearly
- ✓ Explain relationships clearly

Scale diagrams are used to:
- ✓ Show the size of an object
- ✓ Compare the size of one object to a familiar object
- ✓ Summarize information using pictures

Scale: _____ = _____

Creating/Presenting: Presents a solution to a problem using diagrams

Name: _____   Date: _____

_____

Labeled diagrams are used to:
- ✓ Summarize information using pictures
- ✓ Name parts of a picture clearly
- ✓ Explain relationships clearly

_____

TEACHING TIPS...

Labeled diagrams:
- Use to show relationships.

- Use to name parts of an object and to understand relationships, e.g., parts of a plant, food groups, machine parts.

Scale diagrams:
- Useful to develop understanding of size or mass, e.g., to show comparative size of sea creatures.

Use a key to indicate scale, e.g., 1 inch = 1 yard

Creating/Presenting: Presents a solution to a problem using diagrams

Name: _____   Date: _____

_____

Cross sections are used to:
- ✓ Show the difference in appearance between the inside and the outside of an object
- ✓ Show parts of an object that cannot be seen

_____

Cutaway diagrams are used to:
- ✓ Explore beneath the surface of an object
- ✓ Show how to assemble parts of an object
- ✓ Explain the working parts of a model

Creating/Presenting: Presents a solution to a problem using diagrams

Name: _____ **Date:** _____

_____

Cross sections are used to:
- ✓ Show the difference in appearance between the inside and the outside of an object
- ✓ Show parts of an object that cannot be seen

```
┌─────────────────────────────────────────────┐
│                                               │
│                                               │
│                                               │
│                                               │
│                                               │
│                                               │
│                                               │
└─────────────────────────────────────────────┘
```

TEACHING TIPS...

Cross section:
- Use for objects that can be cut open, e.g., piece of fruit.

- Use labels to explain/support diagrams.

Cutaway diagram:
- Use to reveal what cannot be seen from the outside, e.g., underground animal homes, inside a building.

- May also be used for instructions/explanation for assembling machine parts, e.g., bike.

Creating/Presenting: Presents a solution to a problem using diagrams

Name: _____   Date: _____

Did I learn something new?

I enjoyed this unit...

I tried hard...

I found out that...

Evaluating: Reflects on how well the student worked through the process

Name: _____   Date: _____

Did I learn something new?

☹   😐   ☺

I enjoyed this unit...

☹   😐   ☺

I worked well...

☹   😐   ☺

I found out that...

Evaluating: Assesses own involvement with the topic

Name: _____   Date: _____

Did I learn something new?

☹   😐   🙂

I enjoyed this unit...

☹   😐   🙂

I worked well...

☹   😐   🙂

I thought that... _____

_____

_____

_____

_____

_____

_____

_____

Evaluating: Assesses own involvement with the topic

Name: _____   Date: _____

Reflective Journal

Date: _____

I felt _____ when _____

_____

_____

_____

I thought _____

_____

_____

_____

I liked/disliked _____

_____

_____

_____

Evaluating: Reflects on personal participation in the process

Name: _____ Date: _____

Reflective Journal

Date: _____

I felt _____ when _____

_____

_____

_____

_____

I thought _____

_____

_____

_____

_____

TEACHING TIPS...

- Use to focus on the affective domain.

- Students reflect on their response/feelings relating to the problem or task.

- Precursor to diary writing.

Evaluating: Reflects on personal participation in the process

Name: _____   Date: _____

Taking part in a group...

Did I...

- understand what my role was in the group? ☹ 😐 ☺
- carry out my task as well as I could? ☹ 😐 ☺
- have my turn at speaking? ☹ 😐 ☺
- let others have a turn at speaking? ☹ 😐 ☺
- listen while others were speaking? ☹ 😐 ☺
- offer to help at the right time? ☹ 😐 ☺
- offer to help in an appropriate manner? ☹ 😐 ☺
- enjoy taking part in the group? ☹ 😐 ☺
- enjoy working with others in my group? ☹ 😐 ☺

I liked _____

_____

I didn't like _____

_____

I could be a better group member next time by_____

_____

_____

_____

_____

Evaluating: Reflects on personal participation in group

Name: _____   **Date:** _____

I now know a lot about..
_____

Did I understand what I was asked to do?	Did I find relevant resources?
My friends thought...	I worked well when...
To make it easier next time, I need to...	I thought my own idea to...
I liked...	I didn't like...

Evaluating: Reflects on personal participation in the process

Name: _____   Date: _____

Simple Research Strategy

When used in sequence, the following list of blackline masters form a SIMPLE RESEARCH ORGANIZER based on the 6-stage Information Process. Where appropriate, alternatives have been suggested to allow for flexibility in the choice of blackline masters.

This strategy however, would be carried out with extensive modeling and joint class construction.

Defining:
Brainstorming — Concept map
　　　OR
Draws on prior knowledge to brainstorm key ideas
Identifies main ideas (Subheadings)
Organizes focus questions into headings

Locating:
Uses spine/shelf label to identify resources
　　　(Simple catalog searching may be taught within the context of a unit of work as an oral small-group activity)

Selecting/Analyzing:
Lists key words under subheadings (main ideas)
Writes sentences using identified keywords

Organizing/Synthesizing:
Synthesizes selected information

Creating/Presenting:
Presents information in written and visual sequence

Evaluating:
Assesses own involvement with the topic

Research Strategy

When used in sequence, the following list of blackline masters form a RESEARCH ORGANIZER based on the 6-stage Information Process. Where appropriate, alternatives have been suggested to allow for flexibility in the choice of blackline masters.

Defining:
Understands the topic
Draws on prior knowledge/brainstorms — Concept map
     OR
Draws on prior knowledge/brainstorms — Y Chart
     OR
Makes predictions about likely sources of information
     OR
Brainstorming - Concept map
Devises focus questions

Locating:
Uses shelf label from author, title, subject, series search to locate materials

Selecting/Analyzing:
Records bibliographic sources of information
Identifies key words

Organizing/Synthesizing:
Records information—constructs sentences using identified keywords
Categorizes information into a framework of headings

Creating/Presenting:
Presents a solution to a problem using a simple oral presentation
     OR
Presents a solution to a problem using a simple visual presentation

Evaluating:
Reflects on personal participation in the process — Reflective Journal
     OR
Reflects on personal participation in group
     OR
Reflects on personal participation in the process

Index of
Blackline Masters

Organizing/Synthesizing

Creating/Presenting

Evaluating

JENNY RYAN has worked in school libraries as a teaching/library professional since 1980. She co-authored *Information Literacy Planning Overview—ILPO* in 1998 with Steph Capra. In 1999, this work was awarded the IASL/SIRS Commendation for innovative practice in school libraries. Ryan has since written several more books and produced a video and other support materials on information literacy with Capra. She currently consults in education, writing and speaking, particularly in the areas of information literacy and information technology.

STEPH CAPRA is currently privately consulting for Capra Ryan & Associates, based in Brisbane, Australia. She has presented workshops and papers in Australia and internationally on issues relating to information literacy and information technology. She has been a professional teacher-librarian for over twenty years. Capra co-authored *Information Literacy Planning Overview—ILPO* with Jenny Ryan in 1998 and has been writing support materials since that time.

The enclosed CD-ROM includes Microsoft Excel® (v 3.0) files prepared by the authors for your use. These files are saved in Macintosh and Windows versions. The electronic files correspond to printed forms in parts 1 and 2 of the text. To open a file, place the CD-ROM in your computer and then browse the CD-ROM for the file you want to use. Copy the file to your hard drive where it can be opened and modified. Each file name ends in the page number where it first appears in the text. For example **(your CD drive letter):\Windows\K-6\Grade 1 Planning Organizer-23.xls** is a Microsoft Excel® for Windows file that is printed on page 23 of *Information Literacy Toolkit: Grades Kindergarten–6*.

For help using the forms and for copyright information please consult the introduction beginning on page ix of this book. For help using Microsoft Excel® please consult your manual or the Microsoft website at www.microsoft.com.

License Restrictions
You may not and you may not permit others to use the software in any manner that infringes the intellectual property or other rights of the authors or another party.

Limited Warranty and Limitation of Liability
For a period of 60 days from the date the Software is acquired by you, the Publisher warrants that the physical media upon which the Software resides will be free of defects that would prevent you from loading the software on your computer. The Publisher's sole obligation under this warranty is to replace defective media, provided you have notified the Publisher of the defect within such 60-day period.

The software is licensed to you "AS-IS" without warranty of any kind. THE PUBLISHER DISCLAIMS ALL OTHER WARRANTIES, EITHER EXPRESSED OR IMPLIED, INCLUDING, BUT NOT LIMITED TO THE IMPLIED WARRANTIES OF MERCHANTABILITY AND FITNESS FOR A PARTICULAR PURPOSE. THE PUBLISHER WILL NOT BE LIABLE FOR DIRECT, INDIRECT, OR CONSEQUENTIAL DAMAGES ARISING OUT OF OR RESULTING FROM YOUR POSSESSION OR USE OF THE SOFTWARE. SOME STATES DO NOT ALLOW THE EXCLUSION OF IMPLIED WARRANTIES, SO THE ABOVE LIMITATIONS OR EXCLUSIONS MAY NOT APPLY TO YOU. THIS WARRANTY GIVES YOU SPECIFIC LEGAL RIGHTS AND YOU MAY ALSO HAVE OTHER RIGHTS WHICH MAY VARY FROM STATE TO STATE.